2

Merry Christmas
Dave and Karen!

Blessings in the New Year.

Robyn and Gary

What others are saying about *Make Your Heart a Manger*

Christmas is the perfect time for a heart check. We want our homes, our relationships, and our hearts ready to receive the Christ of Christmas. However, this book, *Make Your Heart A Manger*, and the vital and precious truths inside, will prepare your heart to welcome Jesus every day of the year for a lifetime of loving the Savior. *Make Your Heart A Manger* is like unwrapping the heart of heaven and is the perfect gift for everyone you know, and a loving gift to your own heart as well.

~Pam and Bill Farrel, Co-Directors of Love-Wise and authors of over 55 books including bestselling *Men Are Like Waffles, Women Are Like Spaghetti*

How we experience Christmas is determined by the condition of our heart. On these pages, Cherry and Karen explore the condition of the hearts of many of those who were present at the time Jesus was born. By looking at their experience we can learn so much about ours. Read. Ponder. And let Christmas be an opportunity for spiritual growth this year.

~Jill Savage, host of the No More Perfect Podcast and author of *No More Perfect Moms*

Since we celebrate the birth of Christ amongst a variety of people each year, I cannot think of a better inspiration for your Christmas season than Karen Porter and Cherry McGregor's beautiful new book *Make Your Heart a Manger.* Discover the stories of all the people who surrounded the first Christmas, focusing on what was in their hearts at the time. Mary's was a ready heart, but the Innkeeper's heart was too busy. The Shepherds' eager hearts and the Magi's curious hearts were in stark contrast to King Herod's jealous heart. Each story provokes the important question *Where is your heart this Christmas?* These two storytellers not only weave important truths through familiar biblical characters but open the door of their own lives and celebrations in order to spur the reader to a more thoughtful, intentional Christmas. I look forward to adding this to my annual Advent enjoyment.

~Lucinda Secrest McDowell, award-winning author of *Soul Strong* and *Life-Giving Choices*

In *Make Your Heart a Manger*, the authors take their love for Christmas to a new level—and ours too—when they explore the characters of the original biblical account and their responses to that world-changing, soul-altering birth. Readers' hearts will be more ready than ever to welcome the gift of the Christ-child and the endless depth of meaning in this season of wonder.

~Cynthia Ruchti, author of more than three dozen books, including *Restoring Christmas*

Make Your Heart a Manger is the fresh perspective on the story of Christmas we all needed! The very personal way the authors present the unique situations of each person in the story of Christmas will make you realize the commonalities we have with their stories. It is deep enough for enlightenment while being personal enough for application. Looking forward to gifting this as Christmas devotionals!

~Rachel Hunter, Creative Pastor, Grace Church, Houston

The crush of Christmas activities can put the kibosh on your connection time with Jesus. *Make Your Heart a Manger* refocuses your attention on Jesus by revisiting the witnesses surrounding his birth. Be inspired by Elizabeth's faith, Mary's courage, Joseph's kindness, and the Magi's curiosity. Take a cue from the Innkeeper's busyness and the Shepherd's humility. *Make Your Heart a Manger* is an easy read. Use it as a devotional, an advent resource or devour it in a single sitting—but buy a armload of them because it's the perfect gift for every woman you know.

~Robyn Dykstra, National Christian Speaker, Author of *The Widow Wore Pink*

Christmas is all about heart! In this book Karen and Cherry take a fresh look at Christmas with a focus on the heart of the story. Get it today and be encouraged, refreshed, and reminded of what Jesus can do when we encounter Him. Put it on your Christmas list right now!

~Andrea Booth, Pastor, Grace Church, Houston and co-author of *Paper Conversations*

All the cast of Christmas come alive as Karen Porter and Cherry McGregor invite us to understand the depth and heart of Christmas. With beautiful storytelling and biblical relevance, you'll never see Christmas the same.

~Gari Meacham, author of *Spirit Hunger, Watershed Moments, Truly Fed,* and *Be Free; CEO/Founder, The Vine Uganda; podcast host, Gutsy Faith*

This book will ready your heart with joy for the Christmas season. There may have been no room in the inn that first Christmas, but this book will make room in your heart for Jesus and Christmas joy!

~Vicki Heath, National Director, First Place for Health

It has been an absolute joy going through these chapters and with these people from the Bible. Thank you for bringing them to life with fresh perspective. What a way to edify the saints and reach out to the lost all at once. I know readers will delight in the encouragement and even challenges found here. This has been the merriest July for me.

~Kaley Rhea, Christy finalist author of *Turtles in the Road* and *Off Script and Over Caffeinated*

Make Your Heart a Manger

KAREN PORTER
& CHERRY MCGREGOR

Make Your Heart a Manger

Karen Porter
&
Cherry McGregor

Bold Vision Books
PO Box 2011
Friendswood, Texas 77549

ISBN 9781946708-7-86

Library of Congress Control Number 2022945000

Published by Bold Vision Books, PO Box 2011, Friendswood, Texas 77549 www.boldvisionbooks.com

Published in cooperation with Books and Such Literary Agency
Edited by Kaley Rhea
Cover Art and Design by Gabi McGregor
Interior design by *k*ae Creative Solutions
Published in the United States of America.

Bible versions copyright statements on page 134

Dedication

From Cherry

To the love of my life, Craig. Every day, I see in you the heart of Jesus. In your presence, others feel seen and loved. You love people better than anyone I've ever known. Life with you has always been the greatest adventure. Thank you for choosing me.

To my amazing children, Garrett, Gracen, and Gabi. You are my greatest joy. Every day with you is like unwrapping a present from Heaven above. What an honor to be your mom. May your hearts always be open to His heart.

From Karen

To George. Your heart is the best of Christmas and every other season. When we first married many years ago, your calm composure drove me crazy. Now, I want to be just like you. Every day is like Christmas with you.

Table of Contents

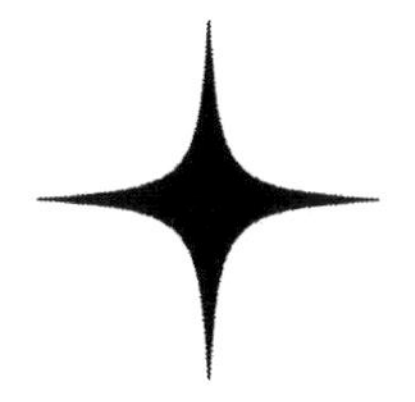

Once in our world, a stable had something in it that was bigger than our whole world.

~C. S. Lewis

Introduction

Christmas. Just hearing the word warms my heart and brings a smile to my face. For my family, no other holiday is filled with so much tradition or celebrated so extravagantly. After I married and spent a Christmas with my husband's family, I realized not everyone "did Christmas" the same way.

I sat in the living room of my husband's childhood home with his parents, his three siblings and their spouses, along with all their children. One by one, names were called, and beautifully wrapped presents were passed out. When the last gift was handed to the last recipient, the chaos began. Everyone ripped into their gifts at the same time. Wrapping paper and bows went flying. Within a few minutes, we were knee high in paper, boxes, bows, clothes, and toys. It was crazy and wonderful.

At our house, Christmas happens at a much slower pace. We pass presents out one at a time and open each one while everyone watches. Will my sons jump around yelling, "Whoo-Hoo?" Will my daughter squeal with delight? Will my husband smile, look my way, and wink, acknowledging the gift is just what he wanted? I search for the perfect gifts in anticipation of those responses.

I wonder if long ago, in a little town called Bethlehem, God felt the same way. He gave the perfect gift wrapped in swaddling clothes and laid in a lowly manger. Was God watching to see how each heart would respond? Would they accept his precious gift? Would they love it? Would they be filled with joy? What would be their heart's reaction? Let's explore each character in the Christmas story and discover their responses and their hearts. Maybe along the way, we'll find our own heart's response to the greatest gift ever given.

~Cherry

****

I love Christmas. The lights and decorations make me happy. When else can you make your house so gaudy and get away with it? I'm like a child—giddy with anticipation of Christmas morning. Maybe because my mother made Christmas so special. We had very little money, but she could decorate an enchanted house with a bag of sugar gum drops.

Yes, I love Christmas.

Some people decorate early, and I don't mind, even if I'm shocked when I go to the mall in August and find Christmas everywhere. I love the joy of family, food, tradition, gathering, giving, and, yes, receiving. The joy is everywhere in the bright colors and glittery displays and in the hearts of people as they bring the celebration into their homes.

When I was a teen, we made an annual trip to a neighborhood nearby where the outdoor decorations were over-the-top. The community had a contest for the best decorated home, and each yard was more extravagant than the one next door. One family's boat was decked out as Santa's sleigh, with a life-sized Santa as captain. Another built a replica of a church in the front yard, complete with stained glass windows and bells. From whimsical to elegant, the decorations and lights lit our souls as we followed the lines of cars down each street.

Each year I unpack decorations that bring joy and tears. A treasured ornament from my grandmother. Hand-blown and hand painted glass Christmas balls from a long-ago trip to Europe. A handmade drawing and a photo of my six-year-old. An ornament with a drawing made from the fingerprint of my toddler. Even the modern décor purchased last year to spice up my tree and change the color scheme. Each item is a treasure that reminds me of Christmas past and promises joy for Christmas future. The season is magical.

A few weeks ago, I found some pictures of my kids depicting the story of Jesus in a Christmas play at church. There is something special about little kids in bathrobes with towels wrapped around their heads.

The Christmas story is why we have explored the characters in the events around the birth of Jesus. We've looked into their lives to discover their heart's condition and to learn how to find the true blessing and meaning of Christmas.

~Karen

****

And while Mary and Joseph were in Bethlehem, the time came for her to give birth. She gave birth to a son, her first born.

The people who experienced the original Christmas story teach us through their heart's response. And they become an illustration for us. When we discover how the attitude and condition of each heart is changed by the coming of Jesus, we learn how to respond to the good news of great joy.

The condition of our hearts sets the tone for our reaction to the birth of Jesus. A damaged or hurting heart will find healing or more pain depending on our reaction to the son of God. We pray you will find belief, obedience, worship, and joy in the greatest gift ever given.

***

She wrapped him in a blanket and laid him in a manger because there was no room for them in the Inn."

Those familiar words we've heard since we were children tell us the story, "They laid him in a manger."

The manger was available and ready to receive the Christ child. The manger did nothing to deserve the honor, but the King of the Universe was placed into the manger's cradle. We too can open ourselves to the Savior by accepting the greatest gift—Jesus Christ.

If only that manger could talk. What would it tell us? We wonder about the hearts of each person who is part of the story.

~Karen and Cherry

Faith is believing when
common sense tells you not to.

~Kelly Finch in *Deck the Halls*

Zechariah

The Reluctant Heart

Leads to The Doubting Heart

An old man shuffled across the courtyard, his heart fluttering and his arthritic knees aching from walking too fast. *He had to tell Elizabeth the news.* As he hurried through the door of his rock-walled house, his rapid breath smothered his shout. "Elizabeth! I've been chosen. Me. The lot fell on me. For the ceremony. Imagine. After all these years, I'll be the one."

Zechariah the priest. His division would serve in the temple this week, and now he alone was selected to enter the Holy of Holies.

On the big day, Zechariah dressed in his ephod. Elizabeth had mended every worn spot and repaired the tassels with new woolen thread. That morning, she cut his hair and massaged his beard with olive oil. He paced around the room. His outer robe hung loose—

his shoulders once strong and wide, now stooped and skeletal. He counted the steps from the door to the wooden table and back again, rehearsing what he would say on this important day.

Maybe I'll quote the Psalm, "May God be gracious to us and bless us and make his face shine on us." Or Isaiah, *"Give ear and come to me; listen that you may live. I will make an everlasting covenant with you, my faithful love promised to David."*

Elizabeth watched. She said nothing, but her smile and sparkling eyes reminded him of her love.

Over the years, young couples brought new babies to him to be blessed and named. On the eighth day, the male children were brought to be circumcised according to the Law of Moses. Zechariah held the child up to God in dedication. Each time, Zechariah wondered, *Why not us Lord? I've been a righteous man. I've walked blamelessly. Why don't we have a child?* An answer never came.

****

Zechariah led the procession from his hillside village through the narrow streets to the steps. He'd been part of this crowd many times, but he had never led as they passed through the gate called Beautiful.

He stopped, and the crowd hushed behind him. The massive columns rose to the roof. He shuddered. The temple seemed bigger and more ominous than ever before.

He spoke the Shema, "Hear, O Israel: The Lord our God, the Lord is one." The crowd repeated the ancient prayer as they followed into the outer courtyard. Jewish men and women followed him into the second courtyard as the ritually pure men separated from the crowd into the third courtyard. Zechariah's priestly division moved into the fourth courtyard and began their duties.

Priests trimmed the lamps on the golden candlesticks, while others found the sacred oil in the supply chamber. Three priests made their way to the great altar to stoke the fire for the evening sacrifice. Each man had an assigned duty for the seven days Sabbath to Sabbath. Zechariah had fulfilled all these tasks in times past, but now he would perform the most honored and sacred duty of the day—enter the Holy Place to offer the evening incense on the golden altar.

He noticed ornate golden vines curving around the opening and hanging from the columns, as if they'd grown there. Gold covered walls reflected sunlight from windows high above.

A trumpet sounded. The other priests finished the preparations and lined up in a straight row. Josiah handed him the smoking vessel filled with the evening's incense. The censer swung in his hands. Quiet filled the room as if no one dared breathe as he reached to part the veil. Hot tears ran down his cheeks, his exciting honor now an awful responsibility. *This is the temple of Almighty God— Who do I think I am?*

In a shaft of light stood a huge man clothed in white. Zechariah gulped. The man spoke, "Do not be afraid, Zechariah, your prayer has been heard."

My prayer? Singular? Ah yes ... The one prayer I've prayed for years and years.

"Your wife Elizabeth will bear you a son, and you are to call him John."

Zechariah fixated on the first part of the message. *Elizabeth would bear a child? Impossible.* He found his voice. "How can I be sure of this? I'm an old man, and my wife is well along in years."

The angel seemed to grow taller, his deep voice clear and resolute, "I am Gabriel. I stand in the presence of God, and I have been sent to speak to you and to tell you this good news."

But Zechariah shook his head and repeated, "Impossible."

Angered, the angel reached out to close the vocal cords in Zechariah's throat.

The being disappeared. Zechariah stared at the spot where the man had stood. *What did this mean? Did he really say ... ? This cannot be.*

Zechariah reversed his steps through the opening, walking past the priests standing in line and into the outer courtyard. He tried to speak to the crowd. No words came when he opened his mouth. Grabbing Elizabeth's hands, he hurried home.

***

The Reluctant Heart

Zechariah abandoned the idea of fathering a child, because God had not answered his prayer for years and years. *Why would God answer now?* He was too old. Elizabeth was too old. He may have wanted to believe the angel. But ...

In spiritual terms, a lack of faith is rooted in reluctance. That questioning, which nags us when our heart says *believe*, but our mind stammers with qualms and misgivings. And when reluctance reaches its fullest place, it becomes doubt—the equivalence of unbelief.

When the disciples faced a storm on the sea, Jesus came to them walking on the water. They were afraid and figured he was a ghost. Peter was brave enough to get out of the boat and walk a few steps before his fear overcame him. Jesus said, "You of little faith ... why did you doubt?" (Matthew 14:31 NIV). Fright and hesitancy begat doubt, and doubt begat unbelief.

Jesus never intended us to live in fear or reluctance, and he knew doubt would make us ineffective and weak. He said, "... if you embrace this kingdom life and don't doubt God, you'll not only do minor feats like I did to the fig tree, but also triumph over huge obstacles" (Matthew 21:21 The Message).

Zechariah was a faithful priest—a man of God. But times had changed, and there was great corruption. Politics were ruthless. Darkness covered the society. He was discouraged. He allowed his reasoning and understanding to build a case for doubt. A reluctant heart produces doubt.

The Doubting Heart

Have you prayed the same prayer over and over? Has the answer never come? Does it seem too late? Does your dream feel impossible now? While God may not give you a child in your old age, he has a purpose for you, and he intends to bring you great joy. You may doubt like Zechariah. You may think you can never be happy without the answer you wanted, but God is God of the impossible.

If you've stopped praying, God has not forgotten. David said, "He hears our prayers."

When God surprises you, don't be reluctant like Zechariah. Pray like the man in Mark 9 when he said, "I believe. Help me with my doubts!" (Mark 9:24 The Message).

Don't be reluctant or you will open the door for doubt to enter your heart. God heard Zechariah and Elizabeth's prayers. He knew their hearts. He hears you, and he knows your heart.

Be ready for the amazing to happen.

Exploring Your Heart

1. Finding My Voice

Zechariah lost his voice and his influence because he was reluctant to believe. Each of us wants to influence others, but our voice can't be heard when reluctance and doubt are louder. When I see my neighbors, who have no connection to God, and hear their heated voices drift across the yard in the evening, I know Jesus could bring peace into their chaotic home. Yet I talk about the weather and kids and school activities. My reluctance is based on what they might think of me if I proclaim the Good News to them. When I see a homeless person begging on the street corner, I hesitate because I've read the stories of con artists. What if the person I see has a real need? Because I'm reluctant, I don't share the love of Christ with them nor give them any help in their trouble.

If I am a Christ follower at Christmas, I must put my hesitance and reluctance aside or I will cultivate doubt and unbelief. If these attitudes grow strong in my life, I will miss the Christ of Christmas. Make a list of at least three ways you can influence others this Christmas without reluctance.

2. Never Quit

Even though Zechariah was old and had served many years, he never quit serving in the temple and following the path of righteousness. If you are discouraged and feel you haven't received answers to your prayers, keep trusting the Lord. Vance Havner said, "Never desert your altar and never forsake your incense, no matter the disappointment—for the angel will yet appear." The Bible says, "The LORD himself goes before you and will be with you; he will never leave you nor forsake you" (Deuteronomy 31:8 NIV).

When Joshua became the leader of the nation of Israel after Moses died, he was about eighty-five years old.

When we hear his age, we think it probably wasn't as old as it sounds because the Old Testament people lived to be hundreds of years old. But Joshua only lived to be 110. The biggest and most important assignment of Joshua's life came in his last 25 years.

How easy it is to accept the status quo and stop trying. Better to relax and let the world go by. *The church will move on without me. The family will understand. I worked hard getting to this point. Surely, I can retire now.* But the Lord said there is still work to be done and promised he would never leave us. The next few years may be the best of your life. Don't miss them by quitting. What if you are starting your last twenty-five years? Will you choose to serve God wholeheartedly? How does knowing God isn't finished with you help you today?

3. Trusting God at Christmas

How can you trust God this Christmas? When I was a girl, my parents went through a rough time financially. They never told me the details, but I understood enough to be careful about asking for too much at Christmas. One day, Mom and I went to the nine-story downtown Foley's Department Store in Houston to see the decorations and window shop.

At the top of the escalator, a mannequin was dressed in a bubble gum pink sweater with fluffy balls on the front. *(I know, I know.)* I squealed with delight. That sweater was everything a pre-teen girl could dream. When I saw the price tag, I pretended the sweater didn't matter. Mom and I enjoyed the rest of our day.

On Christmas morning, I opened my gift to find the sweater, pom poms and all. Somehow, Mother managed the cost of the sweater. Our heavenly father is that kind of loving parent. God is trustworthy even when we can't see what he is doing behind the scenes. When we don't know how a situation could ever change, we can trust God because he will always delight us. He saved the world, and he cares for every detail of life for us, his children. Write a prayer telling God you trust him this Christmas— no matter what your circumstance.

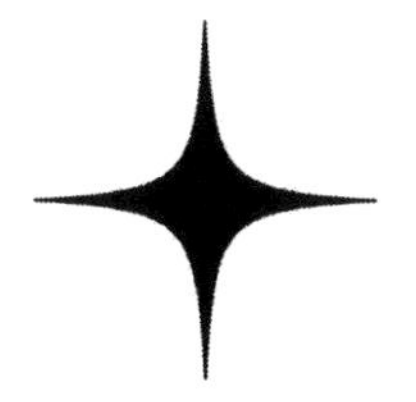

The Reluctant Heart Leads to

The Doubting Heart.

~Zechariah

Expectancy is the atmosphere for miracles.

~Edwin Louis Cole

Elizabeth

The Broken Heart

Leads to The Expectant Heart

Elizabeth stood with the women in the second courtyard. Most of the Jewish men had moved into the third courtyard, and the priests had gone into the temple chamber to perform their duties. She knew Zechariah would soon enter the Holy of Holies to pray. As people prayed in the courtyards, their prayers would mingle with the smoke of the incense and together travel to heaven.

The people.

Maybe now they would stop talking about her. She was old, but she had not forgotten the whispers and patronizing glances. Her prayers as a young woman, begging God for a baby, echoed through her mind. There had been no answer, and she hid her grief as best she could. She shuddered as she turned her attention back to the place where her husband had disappeared beyond the courtyard wall.

From the day he told her about his great honor, a fresh wind of joy had brushed her soul. She was happy for Zechariah. It was his day, a day for celebration. She had washed the linen ephod. As she threaded the wooden needle with new thread to reinforce the seams and hems, she prayed for him. That morning, she had trimmed Zechariah's hair and shaped his beard. Now, she willed her broken heart to rejoice.

When the procession began, birds formed two straight lines in the blue sky. The privileged fowl at the front of each line brought the lines together as if pointing the way for the prayers—the sound of their wings like worship music above the crowd. She had taken her place at the front of the women as they wound their way up the road to Jerusalem. Joyful songs and shouts echoed across the valley.

When Zechariah walked up the magnificent steps to the temple, he'd looked out over the people, held up his hand, and spoke words of blessing. Pools formed in Elizabeth's eyes as she witnessed the man she loved in the place of honor he deserved.

Elizabeth wondered what it was like inside the magnificent temple. "Lord, bless my husband today."

Her friends gathered around her, excited about the big day.

"I've made a special dish of lamb for the celebration tonight."

"I've never seen a man look so happy."

"You look radiant today, Elizabeth. Your joy is shining on your face."

Elizabeth smelled the first scent of the incense coming from the inner courts. She knew it was time for Zechariah's finest moment. He would soon enter to stand before the Ark of the Covenant and intercede for their people. As if on cue, the people began a worship song.

Give praise to the LORD, proclaim his name;

Make known among the nations what he has done.

Sing to him, sing praise to him;

Tell of all his wonderful acts.

Glory in his name;

Let the hearts of those who seek the LORD rejoice.

(Psalm 105:1-3 NIV)

As the song ended, the prayers began. Elizabeth prayed, too. *O Lord, you are our strength and salvation. I have begged you for years for a child and you have not answered; now I am old and cannot bear a child. O God, I beg for peace and acceptance and for a purpose in these last years of my life. Take away my grief and give me joy.*

Darkness was almost upon them when Zechariah came out. She saw his face and sensed the anxiety. What had happened?

When they returned home, he tried to tell her with hand signals and words on a tablet. She knew he'd seen a stunning sight in the temple, but he must be crazy. How could she have a child? Look at them, they were old. The pain of disappointment rushed into her soul uninvited.

****

Elizabeth awoke with her head spinning and her stomach sour. She leaned over the wall and vomited. When the feeling passed, she sat by the fire in the outer courtyard. *Could it be?* Her broken heart quickened with the thought. She would tell no one.

Five months later, she felt the thickness of her abdomen and marveled. She had kept away from the town and the people and worn extra layers when she went to market. If this child was lost, she didn't want the pity of her friends. Better they not know at all.

She heard someone at the door. "Elizabeth. Are you here?"

She recognized the voice of Mary, her friend and relative from Nazareth. *What was she doing here?* As Mary entered the room, the child within Elizabeth leapt. Now, it was clear. What Zechariah had said was true. She was bearing the child who would lead the way for the Messiah.

A few months later when Elizabeth's child was born, she said, "His name will be John."

Family and friends protested, "No one in your family is named John!"

Zechariah wrote on a tablet, "His name is John." With those four words, Zechariah moved from doubt and skepticism to belief, and he spoke again. Elizabeth's broken heart healed.

****

The Broken Heart

Elizabeth's heart was broken, and her dreams were crushed in a way only a childless woman can understand. Thousands of women who have never conceived, or have miscarried or aborted children know the pain and misery she felt. In her culture, not having a child, especially not having a male child, was the ultimate disgrace. She was shamed, pitied, and the subject of much gossip. "Surely," they said, "there must be some gross sin for her womb to be barren."

I walked into my doctor's office. I was 16 weeks pregnant—my first. My husband and I, so full of excitement our hearts were about to burst, waited in the room for the doctor to come in for my checkup. I laid back on the table, eager to hear the rapid thuds on the monitor as the doctor found the heartbeat of our precious little one growing inside. She ran the cold machine over my abdomen. Seconds passed. Minutes. I saw the doctor's brows furrow as she turned and said, "I need to take you to the other room for an ultrasound."

I squeezed my husband's hand and looked for reassurance in his face. We made our way to the ultrasound room only for the test to confirm our fears. Silence. No heartbeat. We cried as we realized the truth of our situation. The next evening, we walked to the hospital to deliver a lifeless baby boy. I remember the heaviness still today. The realization I would leave the hospital with empty arms hurt deeply. A million plans I had already made in my head, a future I had already dreamed, and a lifetime of memories already imagined gone. Dreams crushed. Heart broken.

The Expectant Heart

God had a different plan for Elizabeth. He wants to take our broken hearts and give us a miracle if we will open our hearts to receive the miracle and expect him to work. God had something more amazing for Elizabeth than a house full of children. She would be the one who would raise John the Baptist, the forerunner of the Messiah. She taught him Scripture and told him of his miraculous birth. She was the one—maybe the only one—who understood Mary. She encouraged Mary in a culture quick to condemn.

Just when Elizabeth felt life was worthless, God showed up with great plans for her.

Elizabeth was a mature believer in God. She was from the line of priests, a daughter in the lineage of Aaron. In the gospel of Luke, we learn both she and Zechariah were righteous before God. They walked blamelessly in all the commandments and statutes of the Lord. Despite her years of disappointment at not having children, her faith had grown. She followed God year after year through unanswered prayers. Her faithfulness led to a miracle. She would raise one of the greatest preachers ever known, and she would spend time with the mother of Jesus.

God had a different plan for me. A year later, I found out I was pregnant again. I was filled with immense joy and intense fear. My heart had been broken, but my heart was expectant for a miracle from God. I have three beautiful, healthy children. Instead of working and building a career as I had planned, I let it go to stay home and raise my kids full time. What a privilege.

For several friends of mine, their miscarriages and failed pregnancies didn't lead to babies. Their open hearts led to a different type of miracle—adoption. Wonderful children needing exactly the right family. Their broken hearts healed with the miracle of adoption. God's perfect purpose and his perfect plan.

What about you? God has more planned for you than you could ever imagine. In fact, he has promised greatness for you.

"'For I know the plans I have for you,' declares the LORD, 'plans to prosper you and not to harm you, plans to give you hope and a future.'"

(Jeremiah 29:11 NIV)

Exploring Your Heart

1. Eyes on Him

If your heart is broken and your dreams are crushed, wait on him with an expectant heart, trusting he has a hope and future for you as well. Waiting is difficult. Listening to voices in your head and from the mouths of well-meaning family and friends can be devastating. How do we trust God for a miracle and make our hearts open to receive?

Many years ago, I walked through a difficult situation. I was broken and lost. I didn't know what to do. During this time, God led me to a beautiful passage in the Old Testament. Over the years, it has become my favorite, and repeatedly, God has used it to speak to me. The passage is 2 Chronicles 20. In this chapter, King Jehoshaphat received word a mighty army was coming against him. The situation looked hopeless, and the people were desperate. King Jehoshaphat gathered the people together and asked them to pray. In 2 Chronicles 20:12, Jehoshaphat declared, "We do not know what to do, but our eyes are on you" (NIV).

Those words resonated with me. I didn't know what to do, but I would keep my eyes on Jesus. I would keep believing, and I would keep trusting. I read my Bible. I prayed. I sang worship songs. I went to church. I listened to sermons and messages from great Bible teachers, and I talked with godly friends who encouraged me to keep trusting. I kept my eyes focused on him and seeking him continually. Together, God and I made it through the difficult time.

If you are walking through a difficult time and your heart is broken, open it for a miracle. I encourage you to pray these words to him as many times as they come to your mind. "I don't know what to do, but my eyes are on you." Write the words on a sticky note and hang it on your bathroom mirror, car dashboard, or anywhere you will see it throughout the day. Repeat the words as an affirmation of your absolute trust in him.

2. Trace His Hand

If your heart is broken and you are waiting for a miracle, the wait might last a long time. You may be tempted to give up hope. One of the best actions we can take is to trace his hand. Throughout the Psalms, David traced the hand of God as he walked through difficult times and waited for God to move. "I will remember the deeds of the LORD; yes, I will remember your miracles of long ago. I will consider all your works and meditate on all your mighty deeds" (Psalm 77:11-12 NIV). "Yes, I will bless the Lord and not forget the glorious things he does for me" (Psalm 103:2 TLB).

This exercise of remembering would bolster David's faith for the future. He remembered God's faithfulness in the past and knew he could trust him in his future.

What has God done in your life in the past? What has he done long ago, last year, last month, last week? Think of the defining moments in your life. What are the moments when God showed his power in your life? What are the times when he guided you in a very specific way? What prayers has he answered and what promises has he fulfilled? Take a moment to trace the hand of God in your life.

3. Christmas Miracle

For many, the Christmas season is exciting and wonderful. Maybe for you it is excruciating. Your heart is broken. Perhaps you are missing a loved one, and you don't feel like celebrating the holidays. If this is you, take a moment to reflect on the greatest miracle of Christmas. God himself came as a baby. He gave up the splendor of heaven to reside in human flesh. He was born of a virgin girl, lived a sinless life, died on a cross for our sins, and was raised again. He came because he loves you. Oh, how he loves you. He loves you, and he sees you. He sees what you're walking through. He sees your crushed dreams, and he sees your broken heart.

"The Lord is close to the brokenhearted and saves those who are crushed in spirit."

(Psalms 34:18 NIV)

Christmas traditions are big in our family. We couldn't possibly put up our Christmas tree without Elvis belting "Blue Christmas" and Harry Connick Jr. crooning "It Must've Been Ol' Santa Claus." And what is Christmas morning without Mom's homemade cinnamon rolls and hot chocolate? Make your heart open for a miracle this Christmas by remembering God's work and incorporating it into your Christmas traditions.

Remember the paper garland every kid makes by cutting strips of paper, fashioning them into circles, and stapling them together? This year, I encourage you and your family to find some pretty paper (gold, silver, or whatever goes with your Christmas theme) and cut it into strips. On each strip, write an instance of how God moved in your lives over the past year. Write about a time God moved on your behalf, a time he answered a prayer, or a time you saw him perform a miracle. Staple them together. Put it on the tree, and each year, add to it. It will be an amazing chronicle of God's miracles, answered prayers, fulfilled promises, and his faithfulness. It will remind you of his goodness, his power, and his love.

> "Never doubt God's mighty power to work in you and accomplish all this. He will achieve infinitely more than your greatest request, your most unbelievable dream, and exceed your wildest imagination!"
>
> (Ephesians 3:20 TPT)

Trust him and trust his promises. Elizabeth believed. She responded with great joy as God moved in her life and worked a miracle. Even if your heart has been broken and your dreams crushed, God sees you, and he has a hope and a future for you. A future more exciting than your wildest dreams.

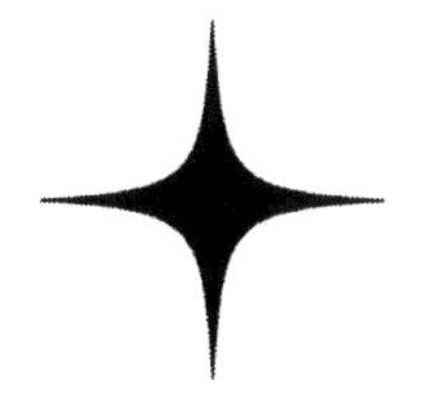

The Broken Heart Leads to

The Expectant Heart.

~Elizabeth

Christmas is not a story of hope. It is hope.

~Craig D. Lounsbrough

Mary

The Ready Heart

Leads to The Believing Heart

Mary climbed the stairs to the roof. She loved the quietness of mid-morning, so different from the loud chatter spilling over from other rooftops in the evening.

She needed to think.

Almost a year ago, her father had announced the negotiations were complete and she would marry Joseph. Their two families united in the special bond when children marry. As she lounged on the mat under the canopy, she ate apricots and dreamed of her wedding day. She'd attended enough wedding celebrations to flash images in her mind. Music, food, games, and processions.

Mostly, she thought of Joseph. Although she'd never spoken with him, she'd seen him working in his father's carpentry shop, and once, when she was at the market, he'd walked by with his arms full. Their eyes had connected for a moment before she lowered her head. He seemed kind and industrious—and mysterious.

Mother and her aunts purchased beautiful linen cloth imported from Egypt. She'd never felt such soft fabric. They were working in the house below to fashion it into a wedding tunic.

Like a fog, an intense light settled around her under the canopy. She gulped with fear and confusion, but something calmed her heart as the vision came into focus.

"Greetings favored woman! The Lord is with you!"

She puzzled over the perplexing words. *Who is this and what does he mean?*

"Don't be afraid, Mary, for you have found favor with God!"

This angel said she would bear a son who would be great. Did he mean the Messiah? She'd heard the reading of Isaiah in temple services, and she remembered some words. "For a child is born to us, a son is given to us. The government will rest on his shoulders. And he will be called: Wonderful Counselor, Mighty God, Everlasting Father, Prince of Peace". The words of Scripture connected with the words of the angel, commingling in her mind. But when they reached her humble and honest heart, she surrendered. And she believed.

She believed it would happen, but she didn't know how. *How could a virgin …* Without understanding, she believed. And her belief brought surrender. "I am the

Lord's servant. May everything you have said about me come true."

As a willing servant, she submitted to God—no matter the pain or the implications.

She pondered the other words of the angel. The Holy Spirit would overshadow her. She recognized this word, *overshadow*. The same word used to describe how God entered the Holy of Holies in the temple. His presence was there. Her body would hold the most holy of all babies—the Son of God.

No way to explain or comprehend it.

****

The Ready Heart

When Gabriel spoke to young Mary, astonishment mystified her as she tried to think of what the angel could mean. But her troubled mind was captured by her believing heart, and her feelings turned to wonder quickly. She believed.

Her family was not prominent or rich. She was to marry a man with a trade, which meant she would work hard all her life, too. And Mary was a girl from Nazareth. The Jews of the time scorned anyone from the Galilee area—especially Nazareth.

Today, some magnify Mary as more than the humble girl from Nazareth, and others neglect to honor her. We should honor her as Elizabeth did when she called her "the mother of my Lord" (Luke 1:43 NLT). Gabriel said she had found favor with God. After considering all the Jewish virgins of the time, God chose her. Her heart was pure, and her faith was uncomplicated—almost effortless. She didn't understand, but she believed. The facts made it hard to understand, but she trusted the angel's words. Her straightforward approach to the extraordinary news was stunning. She wondered how she could bear a child since she'd never been with a man, but she didn't wonder at God sending the One who would save the world.

Mary's heart was ready—already inclined toward the Lord and his Word. Having a ready heart requires preparation to pave the way to hear God. A ready heart clears out clutter and pain and disappointment and anxiety because a ready heart is open, enthusiastically eager to take the next step where God leads.

When I lost my job of more than thirty years as a corporate executive, my first reaction was grief and panic stirred together by the questions about the future. *Why did this happen to me? How will we pay the bills? Can we keep the dream house we just built? Where should I look to find new work? Can we survive?*

I wouldn't say my heart was ready like Mary's because she instantly believed and accepted God's plan. I reacted a lot slower. But over the weeks and months following my job loss, God spoke to me through his Word and helped me understand he would never let me go.

"For he has said, 'I will never leave you nor forsake you.' So we can confidently say, 'The Lord is my helper; I will not fear; what can man do to me?'"

(Hebrews 13:5b-6 ESV)

I read the book of Isaiah, discovering how he would be with me in the days and years ahead.

> "Fear not, for I am with you; be not dismayed, for I am your God; I will strengthen you, I will help you, I will uphold you with my righteous right hand."
>
> (Isaiah 41:10 ESV)

These verses straight from the heart of God, along with the gentle touch of the Holy Spirit, massaged my heart into a ready place. Instead of striving for corporate success, I wanted to follow where he led—even if I couldn't see how it was going to work. My heart went from selfishness and self-promotion to the heart of a servant who was available. Ready.

The Believing Heart

The Messiah would come as a child. The truth filled Mary's heart—she would bear the child who would save the world.

The contrast between Mary's reaction and Zechariah's is clear. She saw the big picture of salvation and believed God could use even her, but he saw the blocks in the road for the miracle and didn't comprehend the significance of his and Elizabeth's part in God's master plan. He didn't understand how God's promises were coming true until after the birth of John. God rewards faith and judges unbelief. She praised God. He was struck dumb.

And she would become pregnant. Not Joseph … The Holy Spirit … And the power of the Most High. The baby born to her would be holy in a way never known before.

The angel gave her a hint of encouragement when he told her about Elizabeth—proof nothing is impossible with God. Only the power of God could make this happen.

Mary's heart turned to God when she heard the news. Not herself. Not even what this news meant for her reputation or whether the news would stop her marriage from taking place. God had promised the Savior many years before, and as God always does, he was keeping his promise.

Through her.

God does not see as we see, and he often picks the unexpected to show his way to the world.

Mary believed. She yielded her will to God's, and God performed a miracle like no other. Mary stored up these thoughts and pondered each one in her heart. The word "pondered" means she put it together like a puzzle. And she concluded God was faithful. She believed. And she was the first to worship Jesus.

Exploring Your Heart

1. Belief Grows

Mary would need her believing heart as she watched him grow. There would be times she misunderstood him, like the time he stayed at the temple when he was a young boy, And other times she worried about him, like in Mark 3 when she and his siblings came to visit. But she never stopped believing. At the wedding in Cana, she told the servants, "Do whatever he tells you to do." She believed. As she watched him suffer and die on the cross, the ponderings of her heart swelled into strong belief. Later, as the disciples waited in the upper room, she was there praying. Her spiritual growth began when she accepted the words of the angel and grew as she saw Jesus live on earth among the people. She saw his kindness and his miracles, and she heard his words. Her belief grew.

I've watched my level of belief grow through the years, too. When I look back at the moments he rescued me, I understand more about how he is my Savior. Remembering desperate situations with finances or health scares always ends with how he healed me and how he brought unexpected resources—and explains how he intervenes in my life. Old sermon notes and Bible study journals illustrate how he has taught my faith to expand. Oh, how I've grown from my old legalistic mindset into grace and freedom. Mary experienced this growth as she watched Jesus become a man and eventually die for the world's salvation. Name at least one way you have grown spiritually.

2. Grace Grows

Mary was condemned by society for a pregnancy out of wedlock. I'm sure the lies about her were painful, but she knew the truth. We might handle the whispers with retaliation or spread a few stories about our attackers. Our natural tendencies might lead us to snap back or get into an argument because the pain of rejection feels like too much. Miracles are sometimes the product of pain. As we grow in our relationship with Jesus, we will let go of the lies and the liars. We will trust God with our reputation and our feelings.

Mary was considered a nobody in terms of social status, yet God favored her and showered his grace on her. God often seeks the unremarkable for his special grace. He loves the humble heart that trusts in his promises and his character. When has God shown grace to you when you were misunderstood?

3. A Christmas Song

Mary sang. Her song is a product of joy, and her desire was to magnify God. "Oh, how my soul praises the Lord. How my spirit rejoices in God my Savior!" (Luke 1:46-47 NLT). She called him God my Savior because only God could rescue her personally and the nation too. She'd heard of the Messiah from the time she could understand, but no one knew when he would arrive.

She praised God and rejoiced in God because she had been chosen, even calling herself a lowly servant girl. "For he took notice of his lowly servant girl, and from now on all generations will call me blessed" (Luke 1:48 NLT). Mary gave him her body. "May everything you have said about me come true" (1:38 NLT). She gave him her soul. "Oh how my soul praises the Lord" (1:46 NLT). And her spirit. "How my spirit rejoices in God my Savior!" (1:47 NLT). She rejoiced in his plan for her life and received his salvation.

Music and songs have played an integral part in my life. From the bee-bop hits of the 60s to classical masterpieces which stir my passion, I love music. The melodies speak to me, but the words reach my soul.

A few years ago, I read a book titled, *The Art of the Almost Said* by Robert Hudson and began writing poetry as an expression of my thoughts. The idea of taking my innermost feelings and expressing them in words brings me joy and helps me express my deepest worship and praise of God. Hudson said, "In both prayer and poetry, we express the same urge to relinquish, to give ourselves away. Writing a poem is a gift to the readers; it is an act of open-handedness, of generosity … Poetry and prayer overlap. They begin and end in silence and in between, they share a common language, not of words, but of perception, emotion, and mindfulness."

Read Hannah's song in 1 Samuel 2:1-10 and compare it to the song of Mary. Now write your own words for your Christmas song as you believe and accept the Savior.

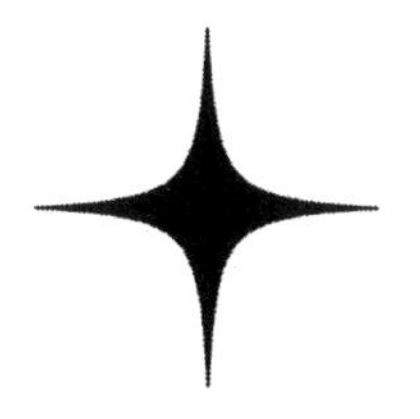

The Ready Heart Leads to

The Believing Heart.

~Mary

My idea of Christmas, whether old-fashioned or modern, is very simple: loving others. Come to think of it, why do we have to wait for Christmas to do that?

~Bob Hope

Joseph

The Kind Heart

Leads to The Obedient Heart

Joseph wrapped his fingers around the handle of the wooden hammer. He turned it over in his hands and fought the urge to throw it across the yard. Instead, he grabbed a nail, and with as much strength as he could muster, smashed it into the table. This table, with its edges still rough and unfinished, was for their new home, and he had been preparing it for months.

Could it be true? Was she really pregnant?

He picked up another nail and pounded it into the wood. A tear slid down his cheek and dropped onto the table. They were engaged. She was his bride.

How could she be pregnant? What had she done?

She had dared to enter his shop, even though they were not supposed to be alone together. She spun an unbelievable tale of an angel visiting her with incredible news. Amazing news. Mary claimed she would be the mother of the long awaited One.

Yet, it was obvious Mary had been unfaithful. Joseph knew his rights. He could have her stoned and be done with this humiliation. No one would think badly of him. "She deserved it," they would say.

Oh Mary!

He knew he couldn't be a part of stoning her. He didn't want to disgrace her publicly either. The kind way would be to break the engagement and quietly walk away. He rubbed the tabletop and picked up another nail but couldn't find the strength to raise the hammer. What was the point? It was over.

There had to be a way out of this mess. He laid his head upon the table, cried, and eventually drifted off to sleep.

"Joseph." He heard a whisper. "Joseph."

Standing before him, a being dressed in white glowed with a light like nothing Joseph had ever seen.

"Joseph, son of David, do not be afraid to take Mary as your wife. For this child within her was conceived by the Holy Spirit. And she will have a son, and you are to name him name Jesus, for he shall save his people from their sins."

As suddenly as the being in white appeared, it disappeared. Joseph realized he had been dreaming.

The angel confirmed everything Mary said. It was

true. She would be the mother of the Savior of the world. He had his answer straight from God's angel. He would marry Mary and do exactly what the messenger had said.

****

The Kind Heart

Joseph. What a man. According to the King James Bible, he was a righteous man. The Message Bible calls him a noble man. He was full of integrity according to The Passion Translation. How hard it must have been for such a man to hear he had been betrayed. Wronged in the most horrible of ways, Joseph didn't respond in anger or revenge. He didn't scream and yell—nor try to get even. He didn't shame Mary in front of their family, friends, and community. Joseph didn't have Mary killed—the ultimate punishment for the ultimate embarrassment.

Even before the angel's visit, even before he knew the truth, he acted one way when the world would give him permission to act another. He would let her keep her dignity and walk away. He would be the bigger man and respond with kindness.

Kindness. *The New Oxford American Dictionary* defines it as the quality of being friendly, generous, and considerate. My grandmother would quote Matthew 7:12, the Golden Rule, and define it as treating others the way you would want to be treated.

Unfortunately, it seems kindness is an attribute our world has in shorter and shorter supply. We sit behind our screens, with keyboards at our fingertips, and speak in judgment over people and their circumstances. We forget *our* mistakes and *our* missteps and pronounce unkind words over others. Our kids have forgotten to look for those unseen and those mistreated to be a friend. Instead, they join in with others bullying those who are different. Have you ever been wronged by someone or treated unfairly? How did you react?

Recently, we celebrated my son's twentieth birthday. He loves a good juicy steak, so our extended family dressed up and went to a favorite restaurant. Our food was delivered and placed before us. As is our custom, we grabbed one another's hands and bowed our heads to give thanks before we ate. We enjoyed our scrumptious meal and our time together. As we were paying the bill, our wonderful server, Salvadore, asked, "Do you guys go to church, and do you try to act like Christians at other times too?"

I laughed and said, "Yes, we go to church, and we try."

Salvadore then told us the worst shift to work at the restaurant was Sunday afternoon. He said no staff wants to work that shift because the Christians who come in after church are the most demanding and unkind people. We all cringed, told him what a great server he was and tried to apologize for *those church people.*

Where have we gone wrong? Where did we lose the basic skill of showing kindness to one another? How can an unfilled water glass or a steak a little too well done warrant such wrath?

Christ followers should be the kindest of the kind. In Ephesians 4:32, Paul says, "Be kind to one another, tenderhearted, forgiving one another, as God in Christ forgave you" (ESV).

God has shown his kindness to us by sending his Son, Jesus, to die for us and forgive us when we deserve death. He loved us so much he gave his Son to pay the price for our sin. We can be kind because God has been so very kind to us.

A mercy like Joseph exhibited came from a lifestyle of kindness. He must have practiced it throughout his life to have displayed such kindness when he felt so wronged. Kindness is a choice. In the book of Galatians, kindness is mentioned as the fruit of the Spirit. Good fruit grows with time and proper care. Kindness will grow when we make a conscious effort over time to be kind. Kindness should be our default reaction in any situation. Perhaps if we practice a lifestyle of kindness like Joseph, we too will develop habits that allow us to respond well when a more serious situation arises.

The Obedient Heart

Joseph was a righteous man. His love for God and the kindness he had in his heart resulted in an obedient heart. Matthew 1:20 says, "after he had considered these things ..." (CSB). Joseph was logical. He thought over the situation thoroughly. He didn't ignore the problem Mary presented; he pondered it. He understood the legal ramifications, and he understood the social dilemma. Yet because he was kind, he was determined to let Mary go quietly. After he considered this, the angel appeared.

Although Joseph was logical and kind, he believed in a God who was supernatural. When Joseph awoke from his dream, he immediately obeyed and took Mary as his wife. God is bigger than our logic and bigger than our situations. Because Joseph loved God and had a kind heart, it stirred an obedience in him to follow God with his whole heart.

Exploring Your Heart

1. Speak Kindness

Do you ever think something kind but fail to say it aloud? In a world full of negativity, one small kind word can make a huge difference.

Proverbs 18:21 says, "The tongue has the power of life and death" (NIV).

We choose our words, and we have the power to kill or give life with our words. They can become like robust fruit or like poison.

Proverbs 15:1 says, "A gentle answer turns away wrath, but a harsh word stirs up anger" (NIV). When we carefully choose our words and choose to speak kindness, we can change our situation and the life of another.

My husband, Craig, is the absolute best at speaking kindness. He is gifted at seeing those who need a kind word, and he's not afraid to speak it. Recently, he was scheduled for a surgery, and the timing of it was important because of our travel schedule. Early in the morning, on our way to the hospital, we received a call from the nurse. His surgery was canceled, and he would need to call the office to reschedule.

I felt irritation and annoyance rise within me, and I wanted to scream. Instead of complaining or being mad at the nurse because of the inconvenience, Craig spoke understanding and kindness to her. Because we were driving, the nurse was on speaker phone, and I could immediately hear a shift in her tone. She was prepared to hear complaining and anger, yet Craig's response left her almost stunned. The nurse was grateful for his kindness in a situation over which she had no control. Craig gave life with his words.

Find someone today you can speak kindness to and share a positive word with them.

2. Be Aware of Those Around You

Harold S. Kushner, a rabbi and author, said, "Do things for others, not because of who they are or what they can do in return, but because of who you are."

Let's be honest, we can sometimes be picky with whom we decide to show kindness. We may limit kind acts to our friends and family, people with authority over us, or people from whom we can attain something in return. But Joseph's lifestyle of kindness reminds us to extend kindness to everyone. Jesus spoke about loving and being kind to our neighbor, our enemy, strangers, and those suffering.

Kindness begins by letting go of our selfishness and opening our eyes to those around us. Look where you are at this moment and notice who is present. It's easy to bury our heads in our phones on public transportation, in restaurants, in lines, at ballgames, even at church. For many of us, it's become a bad habit, and we now have to make a conscious effort to see others.

Jesus saw. For three years of ministry, he looked at others and saw their needs, and he turned no one away. How often are we so busy we miss opportunities to be kind and show the love of God? We must take the example of Jesus, slow down, and see the needs of others.

****

My basketball opponent dribbled down the court as I played defense. We neared center court, and she hesitated. I got in front of her and stood my ground. When I took the charge, I heard a loud pop in my knee, and then came excruciating pain. My anterior cruciate ligament had torn in half, and I needed surgery.

As I woke up from the anesthesia, I knocked on my knee with my fist. *What was this heavy object on my leg?* I'm not sure what I expected, but my teenage self was not prepared to be in a plaster cast from my hip to my toes. I remember it was so heavy. There would be weeks of lugging the heavy cast around on crutches. Thankfully, we could use a wheelchair for those times when crutches were too much of a struggle.

The wheelchair experience was one I will never forget.

People refused to look me in the eye. I was confused at first and then realized it was because of the wheelchair. People didn't see me; they only saw the chair. It hurt. I only had an injured leg. My mom and I made a game out of it and counted how many people looked me in the eye and smiled or said "Hi." For those who did not, we went out of our way to get them to acknowledge me. Wow, what a lesson I learned about not only the disabled but kindness in general. It's a lesson I've carried with me for nearly forty years.

Kindness requires intentionality. We've all heard of random acts of kindness, and they are great. Those unplanned, on the spot, in the moment acts are beautiful, but they do not negate the need for intentionality. Make a choice to show kindness in small ways. Look the checker at the grocery store in the eye, ask about their day, and say thank you. Give up your seat on a bus to anyone—not just the little old lady. Smile at a passerby and say hello. In order to build a lifestyle of kindness, we must plan specific acts of kindness and plan for the random. When we live our life with an attitude of consistent kindness and we open our eyes and become aware of those around us, those opportunities for random acts of kindness don't seem so random. Plan an act of kindness for someone today or plan to perform a random act of kindness—intentionally.

3. Holiday Kindness

During the holidays, it is the easiest time of year to be kind and obedient. For most, it is a happy, joyous season, full of opportunities to share love and kindness.

For many years in our home, we have hosted a small family home group through our church. Every Christmas, we try to do something kind in our community. Some years we have made small gift baskets, loaded up everyone in cars and visited elderly people in our community to sing Christmas carols and give them a basket. Other years, we have bought backpacks, filled them with food, Bibles, socks, gloves, hats, and other goodies. Every family takes a few to give away to the homeless during the holidays.

Here are a few ideas to encourage you and your family to focus on kindness this year.

◆ Find a family experiencing a difficult time and provide everything needed for a wonderful Christmas meal.

◆ Invite someone who is alone into your home to experience the holiday season with your family.

◆ Volunteer at a homeless shelter or nursing home, host a toy drive, or adopt a family to help provide Christmas presents.

◆ Make Nativity Story Trail Mix. You can use the recipe found at www.ahundredaffections.com available with a free printable tag or make up your own recipe. Layer the following ingredients in a mason jar to share at your local fire station and police station or with friends and family.

    - HUGS (LUKE 2:7) Mary embraced Jesus and wrapped Him in swaddling clothes.

    - MINI MARSHMALLOWS (LUKE 2:7) Jesus was laid in a manger and had no pillow for His head.

- ALMONDS & DATES (LUKE 2:4-5) Almonds & dates are native to Israel – food for weary Mary & Joseph as they traveled to Bethlehem.
- PRETZELS (LUKE 2:9-14) Angel wings – Angels declare the birth of Jesus to the shepherds.
- POPCORN (LUKE 2:15) The shepherds traveled to Bethlehem; corn is food for sheep.
- 3 MUSKETEERS (MATT. 2:2) Wise men from the East (traditionally 3) came to worship Jesus.
- STARS (MATT. 2: 2) Wise men followed the star to find Jesus and worship Him.
- GOLD CHOCOLATES (MATT 2:11) The Wise Men brought gifts of gold, frankincense, and myrrh.

We don't have to look very far to show kindness. As we are obedient to show kindness with intention each day, we shine the light of Jesus to a world in desperate need of a Savior. Kindness is love in action. Have the heart of Joseph and be kind to someone today and every day.

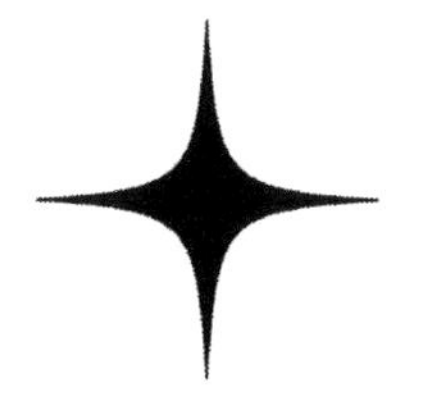

The Kind Heart Leads to

The Obedient Heart.

~Joseph

One of the most glorious messes in the world is the mess created in the living room on Christmas day. Don't clean it up too quickly.

~Andy Rooney

Innkeeper

The Busy Heart

Leads to The Empty Heart

Eli stretched his back and yawned. He'd been up for an hour, and now the sun peeked out behind the clouds. He called out to Sarah, "Don't forget to change the straw in the upstairs rooms." Come to think of it, "Tabitha, we will need fresh water soon." Speaking of fresh, "John, take the cart and go to the market. Our guests will need fresh fruit." So much to do.

Eli looked out the window. Travelers would begin stirring soon. People would fill the streets. His inn had been fully occupied for days. Caesar Augustus had ordered a census to be taken throughout the Roman Empire. People everywhere were required to travel to their hometowns. Bethlehem was full. He had turned many away with, "Sorry, no room."

Just a few nights ago, a young couple had requested a room. The girl was pregnant, her robe doing nothing to disguise her large abdomen. She would give birth at any moment. He gave them the bad news. No room.

Sarah took pity on the young girl, "Eli, can't we do something? They are from Nazareth. They've traveled at least three days. She looks so tired, Eli."

"Sarah, look around. There are tired people everywhere. I can see she's pregnant, but I have problems too. There are others who need my attention. I don't have time to help right now. I'm busy!"

Sarah took his hand. "Please Eli, help her."

He was at a loss. What could he do? The inn was full, but there would be no satisfaction from Sarah if he didn't do something. He had an idea. There was the stable out back. It was meager and barely big enough for the few animals he owned. But it would put a roof over their heads until they could make other arrangements. He offered the young man the stable, and the weary traveler accepted without hesitation. Eli had work to do and guests to serve. He led the appreciative couple to the stable and left them to settle in on their own.

Eli immediately went about his work without a second thought to the couple housed in the stable. *So much to do.*

As the sun rose over the fields, Eli saw his son running toward the inn. *Where was the cart?*

"Abba. Abba!"

"What is it, John? What happened?"

"Is it true, Abba? Is what they are saying true?"

"Slow down, John. What are you talking about?"

"The shepherds, Abba. Everyone is talking about what the shepherds saw. When they were tending their sheep in the fields, angels appeared. Lots and lots of angels. They told the shepherds the Messiah was born in Bethlehem, and the angels said they would find him in a manger. Abba, the shepherds came into Bethlehem and found him just like the angels said. He was wrapped in a blanket and lying in a manger. In our stable. Our stable!"

Eli muttered. "The Messiah, in my stable?" *How could this have happened?*

If only he would have known, he would have gladly offered his own room. He was just so busy. He had missed it. The greatest event to ever take place had occurred in his stable. He could have stood nearby as the King of Glory came. He had missed the Messiah being born right under his nose. He had missed the Savior of the world.

****

The Busy Heart

I missed him too. My days started early. Sons who run cross-country will do that to you. Awake and driving to practice before the sun even thinks about rising. Home in time to get the baby girl out of bed, ready for school, fed breakfast, and out the door. Laundry, dishes, vacuuming. Pay the bills and exercise. Work, work, work. Decorate the tree. Christmas shop. What's for dinner? Back to the school to pick up my daughter. Head across town for double header basketball games. Get home, eat dinner, help with homework, get ready for bed.

In bed, I stare at the ceiling. Guilty. Again. I hadn't spent one minute reading the Bible. I had uttered a few prayers here and there throughout the day, but I hadn't really connected. I kept thinking I'd have a few minutes to sit and spend some time with him, yet those minutes never came. I missed the Savior of the world today. Again.

My life—so full, but empty.

Life can be busy, especially around the holidays. We forget to see not only the big picture but also the beautiful details. The Christmas season is insane. On top of normal activities, there are Christmas trees to decorate, lights to put on the house, gifts to buy, food to cook, school parties to attend, office parties to attend, friend's parties to attend, church parties to attend, gifts to wrap, relatives to visit, and so on and so on. Perhaps you've said, "I'm exhausted just looking at my calendar for the next few weeks." We've all been there.

People are busy. There's no denying that. Books have been written about how busy people can find time for God. Ways to do it quickly and efficiently. Truthfully, if you want to spend more time with God, it all boils down to one word. Priority. Defined by Merriam-Webster as something given or meriting attention before competing alternatives. If we regularly cannot find time for the Lord in our day—let's face the truth—he's not a priority. Ouch. Maybe that feels like a gut punch. It does to me. It's time for us to stop making excuses for not making him most important.

Busyness is not a new problem. People have always struggled with setting priorities. In Revelation 2:2, Jesus says to the church of Ephesus, "I know all that you've done for me—you have worked hard and persevered" (TPT). Then he says, "But I have this against you: you have abandoned the passionate love you had for me at the beginning" (vs. 4). The people were busy working, but loving God was no longer their top priority.

I recently visited the foot doctor because of excruciating pain in the arch of my foot. I was having trouble walking, and by the end of the day, I practically crawled to bed. The doctor diagnosed plantar fasciitis and a heel spur and gave me an injection to help with the inflammation causing the pain. He said I would need to stretch three times (30 seconds each) three times a day. I had been in so much pain, I would have agreed to anything.

Within a couple of days, with the help of the injection and stretching, I was pain free. I was so excited to be walking again. I continued stretching for a few days, but honestly, I wasn't in pain and thought I didn't have time to do all that stretching three times a day. Two weeks later, I was on my morning walk, when I noticed my arch seemed really tight, and I felt a little pain. In my heart, the word *priority* rang out. No pain, no priority. Because I hadn't had pain, I felt I didn't have time for four and a half minutes of stretching in my day. If I wanted to stay pain free, I had to make stretching my priority.

We absolutely must make God a priority. We cannot get so busy we neglect our relationship with him. When something is a priority, you'll make time for it. When was the last time you didn't make time to eat or sleep?

Priority. When was the last time you didn't bathe or get dressed? Priority. When was the last time you didn't pay your bills or breathe? Priority. Time with God must take precedence over every competing alternative in our life. We must make him most important.

The Empty Heart

The Innkeeper's busy heart led to an empty heart. He missed Jesus because busyness juggles the urgent and ignores the important. Let us not get so busy we neglect him. When we are too busy for God we are empty because we don't allow him to fill us with what we need. Especially during the holidays.

> "I pray that you will know the love of Christ. His love goes beyond anything we can understand. I pray that you will be filled with God Himself."
>
> (Ephesians 3:19 NLV)

The Christmas bustle will empty our hearts, but Jesus comes to fill them. Although I love all the celebrations associated with Christmas, I have to remember, it's not about the lights, food, parties, and gifts. It's about Jesus! The Savior of the world. Do not get so busy you overlook something incredible he may have in store for you this holiday. He wants to completely fill your empty heart and, He might have a real God encounter waiting just for you.

Exploring Your Heart

1. Time for God

Busy people live by a schedule. I have a large write-and-wipe calendar by our back door with everyone's color-coded schedule. At a glance, I can see what is happening for the day, the week, and the month. I know most people make their calendars digital, but for me, I like seeing a visual calendar several times a day as I go in and out of the house. It keeps what needs to be done in the forefront of my mind. Life would be chaotic without it. Because I need a schedule, I find it important to have a daily routine, especially regarding time with God. I plan for moments with him.

Luckily for us, God doesn't care *when* we sit with him. He just wants to be with us. Do you need to set your alarm a little early and get up to start your day with Jesus?

"The steadfast love of the Lord never ceases;
his mercies never come to an end; they are new
every *morning*; great is your faithfulness."

(Lamentations 3:22-23 ESV emphasis mine)

"Let the *morning* bring me word of your
unfailing love, for I have put my trust in
you. Show me the way I should go, for to you I
entrust my life."

(Psalm 143:8 NIV emphasis mine)

"In the *morning*, LORD, you hear my voice; in the *morning* I lay my requests before you and wait expectantly."

(Psalm 5:3 NIV emphasis mine)

Or maybe you are like my father who says, "If God had wanted us to see the sunrise, he would have made it later in the day." If mornings do not work for you, there is good news. God can be found in the evening too.

"Arise, cry aloud in the night at the beginning of the *night* watches; pour out you heart like water before the presence of the Lord ..."

(Lamentations 2:19 NASB1995 emphasis mine)

"The way you counsel me makes me praise you more, for your whispers in the *night* give me wisdom, showing me what to do next."

(Psalm 16:7 TPT, emphasis mine)

"At each and every sunrise we will be thanking you for your kindness and your love. As the sun sets and all through the *night*, we will keep proclaiming, 'You are so faithful!'"

(Psalm 92:2 TPT, emphasis mine)

Decide if you are a morning person or a night person or even a middle of the day kind of person. Commit to meet with God at one of those times for the next month each and every day.

2. A Place and A Plan

Along with a scheduled time to meet with God, it can also be helpful to have a set place to meet him. When we encounter God in the same environment every day, we will begin to long for the space, and it becomes holy ground. A friend received a terrible diagnosis which required immediate surgery. She told her doctor, "I need to go home first to sit in my place of prayer and consult God." Your quiet-time space becomes a sacred spot for connection with God.

A plan is also a good idea when making time for God. A plan keeps us focused. You can do a Bible reading plan, work through a devotional book, journal, participate in a Bible study. Find a plan that will keep you engaged daily.

3. Making Christmas Matter

During the Christmas season, when we are at our busiest, it is good to have a time, a place, and a plan. Put it on your calendar and seek him daily. Look for unique ways to slow your pace and find the real reason for the season.

- Read the Christmas story in Matthew 1:18-2:18 and in Luke 1:5-2:20 every day in December.

- Listen to Matthew and Luke on audio as you put out your nativity scene.
- One year for Christmas, I told my young children I wanted them to put on "a play" of the Christmas story. What I got was one of my favorite gifts ever. It was a precious little play, complete with bathrobes, stuffed animals, and yardstick staffs. To hear them telling the story of the birth of Jesus filled my empty heart for the entire season. Ask the little ones in your life to put on a Christmas play this year.
- Take the time to send a Christmas card with a letter to a missionary. Many missionaries cannot be with extended family during the Christmas season. A letter of appreciation and prayers would be a welcome surprise.
- When your family is together, share stories about your salvation. If applicable, have grandparents tell their stories as well. Share personal stories about faith, redemption, and life change.

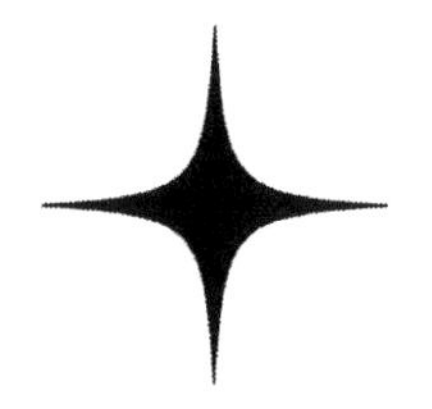

The Busy Heart Leads to

The Empty Heart.

~The Innkeeper

The good news of great joy changed the course of every silent night to come.

~Alicia Bruxvoort

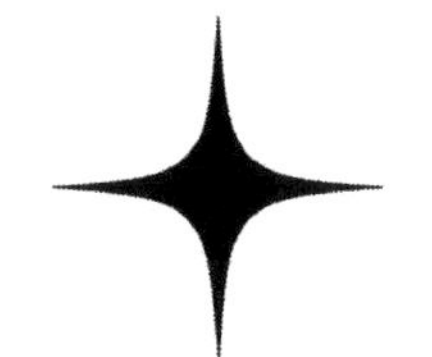

The Shepherds

The Eager Heart

Leads to The Full Heart

Axel leaned against a grassy knoll near the fire. As the sky grew darker, the lights in the sky twinkled brighter on this clear night. He had considered the heavenly formations for years—the moon and stars at night and the sun during the day. He knew the patterns of nature and weather, but it was always the night sky which convinced him of Creator God. Uncle Hiram often quoted the great King David. "You made him ruler over the works of your hands; you put everything under his feet: all flocks and herds, and the animals of the wild, the birds of the sky, and the fish in the sea, all that swim the paths of the seas."

His uncle always ended the recitation with a flourish of his arm and a booming voice, "O LORD, our Lord, how majestic is your name in all the earth!"

Axel's father said, "The way of the shepherd is firmly set and follows the pattern of parents and grandparents before us. We belong to the sheep, and the love and respect for the land is inherited. Each day has no beginning and no end—the sun rises and falls, and the seasons come—and the hours are filled with little unnoteworthy tasks. And then we do it again."

Axel had always been eager to learn, and the words of his father and uncles were part of his straightforward belief in the one true God of Israel as the creator and sustainer of life. Even in his thirst for knowledge, he'd never discounted or regretted his life as a shepherd. The beauty and the order gave him confidence. Nothing ever gave freedom or a feeling of purpose than when he worked the flock.

He spoke to God in the night and felt a burning in his heart as he felt the love of God deeply.

Not that anyone cared what he thought or believed. He had gone into the city earlier in the day, longing to see the great temple, but no one would allow him near the huge structure. His job with the animals made him unclean according to their rules, and he left town feeling rejected and alone. But now on the hillside with the silver wet dew, he felt God's quiet touch and rested in peace. He stretched out, listening to the sounds of a harp played by another shepherd on the hill. He recognized the feeling of timelessness and the humbling sensation of carrying on something bigger than himself.

Then the sky opened in a way he'd never seen before. One angel appeared in the opening, saying, "I have a glad announcement." As soon as he shook his head to see if he was dreaming, a chorus of bright beings joined the one angel in a magnificent sound, "Glory to God in highest heaven, and peace on earth to those with whom God is pleased." Then, as if the angel could see his dazed mind behind his astonished face, the angel said, "Don't be afraid."

He relaxed as the angel continued, "I bring you good news that will bring great joy to all people."

***

The Eager Heart

Shepherds have been called the most famous anonymous people in history. The forgotten silent majority who work the sheep. No one knew their names then, and no one knows their names now—even though their story has been told to millions.

Yet in the practical way of life—the daily chores of mending fences, finding good pastures, caring for the animals. According to James Eubanks in his book *The Shepherd's Life,* the shepherd has time to "see a thousand shades of green." These sheep herders were outcasts in society and never associated with religious people. But they were smart in a practical down-to-earth way. They were not easily fooled by fancy words or fast-talking salesmen. They were hands-on men and women who knew how to care for the animals, no matter what danger lurked nearby. Their lives were not filled with fantasy or frills and perhaps not even dreams of a different life.

They heard the angels say a Savior was born. Not a judge or a soldier or a reformer, but one who would rescue. And the shepherd knew it was for him, too. He was eager to know more about the One who would rescue him from the problems of life and the nagging feeling there was more.

The angels also said peace. Shalom. The shepherd heard a nuance in the word—more than no war. This peace was God's peace and would bring healing and salvation.

None of the shepherds seemed surprised or concerned about the angels appearing in the sky. They didn't balk at the idea of the world needing a Savior. They believed and celebrated by worshiping God.

If we watch the world with an open and eager heart, he will be evident. If we look into the details of creation with a hunger to know more, he becomes more real. If we sit still and listen, he speaks. If we read his Word enthusiastically, he teaches us. Each time you open your heart with eagerness, you will know him better.

The Full Heart

The shepherds gathered on the hillside, believing what they heard. They left the field to go into Bethlehem to worship the One who had been promised. Their eager hearts led them to the Savior, who filled their hearts with joy and meaning and purpose. If you feel empty, it may be because your heart is closed instead of eager to hear the good news.

Exploring Your Heart

1. Immediate Obedience

They followed the words of the angels with immediate obedience. Martin Luther once said, "A true believer will crucify, or put to death, the question: 'Why?' He will simply obey without questioning." If these shepherds had waited until they'd had time to discuss it and research the possibility of the angel's message, they might have missed the baby in the manger.

How can we be more immediate in our obedience to God? First believe him and what he says. Develop the habit of trusting his words even when you can't see any evidence. Second, fall in love with Jesus so deeply that you won't question his instructions. Third, listen to his commands and obey rather than making excuses. Read Galatians chapter three in the Message Bible. Memorize the line in verse 11 that says, "The person who lives in right relationship with God does it by embracing what God arranges for him." Repeat this verse often to remind yourself of God's loving plans for your life and commit yourself to immediate obedience.

2. A Story to Tell

The shepherds ran to Bethlehem, looking for the promised Messiah in the stables of the town. Imagine the joy and praise in their hearts from the moment they heard the angel's words, "Glory to God in highest heaven, and peace on earth to those with whom God is pleased"

(Luke 2:14 NLT). When they found the child lying in the manger, they continued praising and told everyone of the Christ. Then they went back to their jobs on the hill-sides, watching the flock. But they were changed. Now they praised and glorified God. Now they had a story to tell. Their lives were renewed and enlightened. God had come to earth to save His people. And these shepherds saw it all.

Seeing and praising Jesus changes you. A few years ago, our family and the people of a new church plant in Canada worked together to raise money for a water well in Haiti. The need for fresh water there is critical. After the well was finished, a 7.0 magnitude earthquake ravaged the country, and the tiny town where the well had been placed was the epicenter of the earthquake. According to World Vision, more than 250,000 people died and 300,000 were injured.

Buildings and fields and roads were destroyed, as evidenced by overwhelming piles of rubble. When daylight arrived, people in Léogâne dug out of the debris desperate for shelter, food, and water. Someone ran to the well to work the handle and the people watched as he pumped out fresh water. The well was not damaged, and the town rejoiced. The new church in Canada praised God and our family and friends celebrated because of the goodness of God. Some family members even went to Haiti to help in the devastated area. They saw the well. And like the shepherds, we've told everyone of God's miracle.

When have you seen God's miracle and how have you praised him? You have a story to tell.

3. The Reason for Christmas

This Christmas let's consider the plan of God, who sent his only Son to become a human and ultimately pay the price for our sins. The need for a Savior began when Adam and Eve sinned against God and passed a sinful nature to everyone born since then. We are prisoners of sin. The only cleansing of sin is death. But the reason Jesus came was to provide a different way for us to be free from sin and find life eternal. He came to earth. He lived a sinless life. He died on the cross instead of you and me—paying our debt and providing a way out of death. No wonder the amazed angels saw the Creator become the creature, and the Word became a speechless baby. The gift of life is free. Have you accepted the Savior's gift personally?

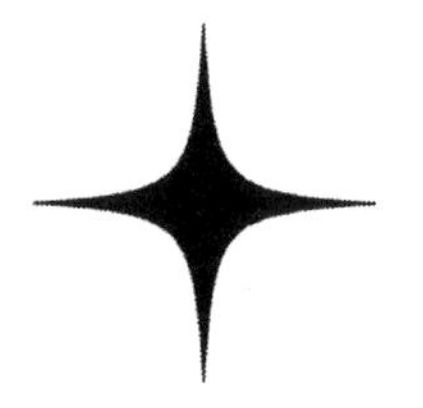

The Eager Heart Leads to

The Full Heart.

~The Shepherds

Christmas, my child, is love in action. Every time we love, every time we give, it's Christmas.

~Dale Evans

Magi

The Curious Heart

Leads to The Worshiping Heart

Melchior stepped out into the cool evening. He pulled his cloak a little tighter around his shoulders and looked east. There it was again. A bright light appeared not too far above the horizon. It was the third night in a row he'd seen the strange sight. He wasn't sure what it was or what it meant.

His grandfather had taught him to study the skies as they spent hours lying in the field searching the vast heavens. He told stories about the stars—and pointed out the pictures the stars made if you looked hard enough. The lights in the sky often correlated with events in the natural world, showing when to plant, when to gather fish, when to harvest, and when to hunt. He explained to Melchior how the gods communicated with the movement of the planets or stars.

Those nights with his grandfather had sparked interest and curiosity, which grew within him.

Melchior looked again to the east. This light was different. It was brighter and lower in the sky than any other. And it was new.

Gaspar and Balthazar called his name as they ran up the road. "Do you see it, Melchior? It's there again."

"I see it, Gaspar. I cannot take my eyes off it. It seems to pulse almost as if it's breathing. What do you think it is?"

"A star, perhaps. It's so unusual. What do you think it means?" Balthazar gazed at the sky while he spoke. "I've been looking over the ancient writings to discover any history of the light or any possible meaning. In the writings of Daniel, our chief wise man many years ago, there is a discussion of a coming Jewish king.

Melchior said, "And remember the story of the three young Hebrew men who were thrown into the fiery furnace? None of them were burned because the King saw a fourth man walking in the fire and declared him the Son of God. Isn't that a prediction of the Jewish Messiah?"

"The descendants of Daniel are watching for him to be born and called the Star of Jacob. Maybe this star is announcing him?" Balthazar said.

Gaspar said, "All I know is this light is so unusual, I think it is important. Do you see how it moves? As if it beckons us to follow it."

They gazed at the light in silence.

"Let's do it, Gaspar."

"Do what?"

"Let's follow the star and see where it leads."

****

The Curious Heart

The wise men were most likely astrologers and curious by nature. Scholars believe they traveled from Babylonia. Though these men were Gentiles, Babylonia had a large population of Jews. When an unknown light appeared, the wise men sought information about it. Their curiosity led them to search all sources, including the Jewish texts of the exiles who lived there.

In the Old Testament, the prophet Balaam said the Messiah's arrival would be marked by a bright star (See Numbers 24:17-19). The texts of Daniel would most likely have been passed on to the Magi. They may have found other passages also speaking of the Star of Jacob. Perhaps they sought wisdom from the Jewish religious leaders.

Is it possible they knew to follow the star because of the faithfulness of four Hebrew exiles taken captive hundreds of years prior? (See Daniel 1) Had they learned of the coming king because 500 years earlier, Daniel had the boldness to share his faith and hope found in the one and only true God? Had the stories of Daniel's courage been passed down to these Magi? At some point, they gathered enough information and believed enough to follow their curiosity toward the star. They loaded their caravan and began the approximately 1150 mile journey. According to Ezra 7:9, this journey would take around four months.

God has given us all a curious nature. We seek purpose for our lives and meaning for circumstances we don't understand. Deep down, we have an emptiness which needs to be filled, and we spend our life trying to satisfy the longing and hunger for more. Some try power, wealth, people, drugs, or alcohol. But the hole is God shaped, and only he can satisfy the hollowness.

When my daughter Gabi was three, she loved to play hide and seek. I closed my eyes and counted slowly to ten. When I opened my eyes, I could see her peeking out from behind the curtains, but I pretended not to see her and began my search. I looked in ridiculous places like under the small pillow on the chair. I opened and closed drawers and looked behind the dog. During my search, I could hear Gabi giggling as she waited to be found. After a few moments, I would feign exasperation and say, "Where is Gabi?" She would pop out from behind the curtain with a huge grin and say, "Here I am, Momma, here I am!" I would hug and tickle her, and she would want to play again. So I began slowly counting to ten. If you've ever had a three-year-old, you know it's a never-ending cycle.

Seeking God is like playing hide and seek with a three-year-old. God wants to be found. There are more than 145 verses in the Bible telling us to seek him and to seek his face.

Deuteronomy 4:29 says, "But if from there you seek the Lord your God, you will find him if you seek him with all your heart and with all your soul" (NIV).

Jeremiah 29:13 says, "you will seek me and find me when you seek me with all your heart" (NIV).

Matthew 7:7 says, "Ask and it will be given to you; seek and you will find; knock and the door will be opened to you" (NIV).

Psalm 105:4 says, "Look to the Lord and his strength; seek his face always" (NIV).

This need to seek God continually is a recurring theme in Scripture because life can get dark and massive storms can arise. Anyone who has walked through a difficult circumstance has probably asked, "God, where are you?" Much like me, with my eyes closed and counting, I couldn't see my hiding Gabi.

The Worshiping Heart

As the wise men learned more of God, their curious hearts led to the Savior. They recognized Jesus for who he was, and their knowledge caused them to fall to the ground and worship. They opened their treasures and worshiped him by giving gifts of gold, frankincense, and myrrh. When they saw Jesus, they were forever changed. They came face to face with the long-awaited Savior and were overjoyed. It no longer resonated only in their minds, but now also in their hearts. Jesus does that. His presence changes us. When we meet him, we are completely transformed. Their curious hearts led them to find the greatest gift ever given to the world.

When we set our hearts and minds to seek the face of God, we find him, and our hearts are so overwhelmed we worship, and we are changed forever.

Exploring Your Heart

1. Seek His Face Continually

Reading the Bible is the starting point for having a seeking, curious heart. As we read his Word, God speaks to us. He tells us who he is and what he is like. He reminds us how much he loves us and how valuable we are to him. His Word gives instructions and tells us how to live in a way pleasing to him. But seeking him goes beyond reading our Bible.

1 Chronicles 22:19 says, "Now set your mind and heart to seek the Lord your God" (ESV). To set your mind and heart is to make a conscious effort to direct your attention toward God. So often we go through life

mentally coasting through our day. But when we decide to set our mind and heart on him, we focus our attention on seeing his presence. We seek a personal relationship with God that is vibrant, real, present, deep, and intimate.

To set our mind and heart on him is to desire him the way David speaks of in Psalm 63:1. "O God, You are my God. Earnestly I seek You; my soul thirsts for You. My body yearns for You in a dry and weary land where there is no water" (BSB). Seeking God means waking up every day and speaking with him, listening for a word from him, consciously looking for signs of his presence throughout the day, and paying attention for signs of his love. It's desiring him so much you feel as if you are in a desert in need of water. You crave more and more of him day by day and minute by minute.

Today, set your mind on God and acknowledge him throughout the day. Speak to him and include him in your day. Ask him questions. Ask for guidance. Thank him for the little blessings you receive during the day. Pray for people you encounter. Listen for his prompting. Act as he directs.

2. Wise People Still Seek Him

The wise men left everything behind and sought the meaning in the new light in the sky. They set their minds and hearts on seeking God. When they arrived in Jerusalem, they asked, "Where is He who has been born King of the Jews? For we saw His star in the east and have come to worship Him" (Matthew 2:2 NASB1995).

The wise men may have been discouraged at the answers they received. They had taken an incredibly long journey and expected to find the King of the Jews. However, they were met with leaders and officials troubled by their questions, and no one was willing to join them in seeking the King of the Jews. Yet, as they began their journey again, they were filled with great joy as the star led them in an uncharacteristic move from north to south, directing them to Bethlehem.

Like Gabi peeking from behind the curtain, God is waiting to be found. In nearly every passage where the Scripture says to seek him, this promise follows: you *will* find him.

"Whoever would draw near to God must believe that he exists and that he rewards those who seek him."

(Hebrews 11:6 ESV)

What a beautiful promise. God himself is our reward. It's his greatest desire to be found. He wants you to seek him, and he wants to say, "Here I am. Here I am."

Memorize Jeremiah 29:13, "You will seek me and find me when you seek me with all your heart" (NIV), and Psalm 105:4, "Look to the Lord and his strength; seek his face always" (NIV).

3. Christmas Worship

As you seek Jesus this Christmas season, worship him as the Magi worshiped. Worship him with gifts. I read a story about a little boy who asked his mother, "If Christmas is Jesus' birthday, why do we get all the gifts?" What if you gave Jesus a gift this year? What gifts do you offer? How can you honor him?

Have you ever asked someone you love what they would like for their birthday? My husband asks me months in advance. Consider asking Jesus what gift he would like for Christmas and open your heart to hear what he would say.

Does he want you to give to others? In Matthew 25:40, Jesus tells us that when we give to others, it's as if we are giving to him. "I tell you the truth, when you did it to one of the least of these my brothers and sisters, you were doing it to me!" (NLT). When we serve others with our gifts, our talents, our time, and our love, we are actually serving and loving Jesus.

The Magi brought extravagant gifts to Jesus. Gold, Frankincense, and Myrrh were costly and rare. Don't be surprised if Jesus asks for something extravagant and possibly sacrificial. Embrace it and let your gift to Jesus be lavish as well. When you feel you know the gift Jesus would like, give with a worshiping heart, and let the recipient know it's from Jesus.

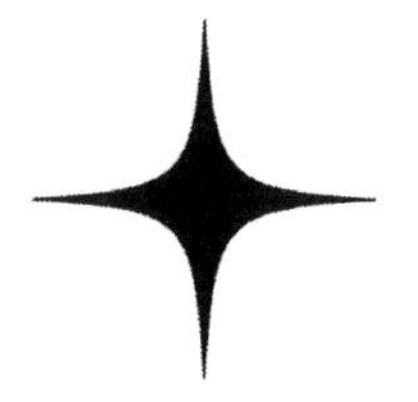

The Curious Heart Leads to

The Worshiping Heart.

~The Wise Men

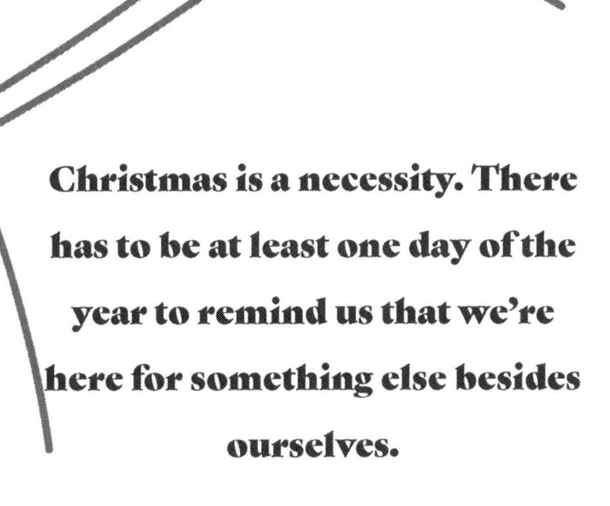

Christmas is a necessity. There has to be at least one day of the year to remind us that we're here for something else besides ourselves.

~Eric Severeid

Herod

The Jealous Heart

Leads to The Destructive Heart

Stretching to seem tall and trying to look regal, Herod came through the arch into the courtyard. He was to meet with the Roman magistrate this morning. He studied the trays of food and goblets of drink. Everything needed to be perfect. He would ask for more power and money today, so the Roman needed to feel important.

He spoke aloud, "I know the Jews hate me even though I've tried to appease them, but why do these Romans hate me? I've followed their directives. Done their bidding."

He noticed the hand crafted and intricate designs in the layers of robes flowing from his shoulders. *It doesn't matter. I hate them all too. They'll never outsmart me.*

A servant bowed low. "My Lord, a caravan of Magi have arrived from the Far East. They've asked to see you."

Herod brushed the slave aside. "I have no time for travelers. Tell them to wait."

Another servant entered. "My King, the Roman magistrate has sent this message. He will not come today because of an urgent matter before his court. He will try to come tomorrow."

Herod spat. "How dare these Roman dogs. What could be more important than me?"

He shouted at the astonished servants. "Tell the travelers I'll receive them."

The grandeur of these regal visitors floated into the room. Herod was instantly jealous of their gold threaded robes and suspicious of their nobility.

One said, "Where is the newborn King of the Jews?"

Fear rose in Herod's mind. *I was appointed king but a king born …*

The second stranger added, "We saw his star as it rose."

Herod remembered how the scribes and Pharisees ranted about the Star of Jacob from the Torah and the great light as foretold by the prophet Micah. He'd never paid much attention to them before. But now …

The third and most imposing visitor said, "We have come to worship him."

Herod was furious, but he held his tongue. "Please wait while I consult my priests and the teachers of the religious law."

As he hurried from the room, his frantic thoughts shook him to the core. *This can only be the Messiah. I have to stop this now.*

"Where is the Messiah supposed to be born?" He stood before the leading priests and teachers of religious law.

In unison, they chorused, "Bethlehem in Judea." One began quoting from a prophet, "And you, O Bethlehem in the land of Judah … a ruler will come from you …"

Herod hardly heard the rest as he devised his plan.

As he entered his royal court where the kings from the East waited, he asked, "When did this star appear?" Storing their answer in his mind, he spoke with feigned kindness. "Go to Bethlehem and search carefully for the child. And when you find him, come back, and tell me so I can worship him, too."

****

The Jealous Heart

A tyrant in every sense of the word, Herod bullied everyone—his wives, his servants, and the people of Israel. His nine wives usually complied easily, especially after he executed the one who dared defy him. His servants stepped lightly around the palace, hoping not to arouse his anger. But the people of Israel were not as easy.

He'd built a magnificent temple for them, yet they still called him a half-Jew. He restored and rebuilt monuments and theaters and even expanded the temple mount.

But they didn't believe he was sincere, nor did they give him the honor he desired. So Herod intimidated them with his rules and decrees. He collected enormous taxes and damaged the economy. Under his rule, the people were dominated and beaten down. No one felt his oppression more than the religious leaders.

Herod's jealous heart played a role in his tyrannical rule of Israel. He pushed for more and bigger and better, and pride drove him to believe no one could best him. Ego and envy led him down the path of lies and murder. Pride ruled him, and the ruler of pride is Satan—the king of liars and murderers. Herod's jealousy would ultimately lead to his destruction.

The Destructive Heart

His success was unrivaled and his genius unequaled. Herod renovated Zerubbabel's temple, known as the second temple. It had fallen into disrepair and became a disgrace to the Jews who loved God. His renovations were grand, and, with great flair, he added golden walls, courtyards, and new altars. He hoped to gain the favor of the Jewish subjects by giving them a beautiful temple for worship. Historians say he put more than 10,000 men to work for the restoration as he doubled the size of the previous temple and surrounding mount built by Solomon.

On a coastal site north of Jerusalem, previously an insignificant place, Herod developed Caesarea Maritima, a huge harbor to accommodate more than 300 ships using an unusual material which hardened underwater. He built a seaside palace with a freshwater swimming pool and a ten-mile-long aqueduct to bring water to the city. For the city's entertainment, he constructed a 3,500-seat theatre and a hippodrome for Roman competitive sports. Herod also created the fortress at Masada with renowned palaces and fortifications and the palace and place for his tomb at Herodium south of the city of Jerusalem. Part of Herodium is below ground for protection, and inside the fortress is Herod's magnificent castle, including gardens, courtyards, and bathhouses.

Though he had built these colossal building projects throughout Israel, he tore the fabric of Jewish society and religion and burdened the life of every Jew in the nation with his tyranny and taxation and bullying.

Herod's destructive pride was born in possessiveness. He wanted to be accepted by both Romans and Jews. He pretended to be Jewish as he played the role of Roman ruler. He didn't please either group because of the deception and ruthless way he dealt with others. His genius abilities to build amazing structures made him feel he had all the answers. If something went wrong, he could not admit he was wrong or ask for help. His jealous heart became willful and stubborn as he drove others away and destroyed himself.

Exploring Your Heart

1. Trust God

Jeremiah said, "Cursed is the one who trusts in human strength and the abilities of mere mortals. His very heart strays from the Eternal" (Jeremiah 17:5 The Voice). When we rely on our personal skills and talents and abilities to make our mark on this world, fear and distrust and scheming plans fill our minds and hearts. We must learn to depend on God alone for our success—and our peace.

Herod depended on himself. He knew enough about Scripture to recognize the baby born as King was the answer to God's promise. His first question to the priests and religious leaders was where the Messiah would be born. For Herod, the possibility of the King of Kings was a threat, not a joy. God's greatest gift became Herod's greatest peril—because he lived in his own strength alone.

When have you relied on your talents and skills instead of God?

2. Taking My Eyes Off Myself

When the wise men didn't return, Herod panicked about a new king being born. He had fought every day to be king and remain king and was determined to destroy the one *born* king. He calculated the time and ordered every male under the age of two be killed.

But the story of Herod's heart is sadder than his choice to murder innocents. His jealous heart led to pride, which kept him from finding the Messiah and ultimately led to his personal destruction. He could not take his eyes off himself, and his smug self-interest to consider the possibility of God sending salvation to mankind. The Pax Romana was supposed to bring peace, but even though the Romans allowed the Jews to continue their worship practices, they charged high taxes and carried law and order to the extreme. Herod was the puppet *king*. His pride made him miss Jesus, who didn't come to overthrow Rome or start a rebellion. Jesus' kingdom is found in the hearts of men and women who humble themselves before God.

His prideful heart led to hostility big enough to commit a crime so heinous. The Old Testament Proverbs warn of the damage pride causes.

"When pride comes, then comes disgrace."

(Proverbs 11:2a NIV)

"The LORD detests all the proud of heart. Be sure of this: They will not go unpunished."

(Proverbs 16:5 NIV)

Pride is selfish and self-sufficient. *I can do this without God's help.* Name one of your talents or skills and describe how it could become a source of pride. Ask God to help you use your gifts powerfully and yet stay humble. Make a list of practical steps you can make to take your eyes off yourself.

3. Eliminating Christmas Jealousy

Even though pride can be positive when expressed as self-respect, appreciation, and confidence, it can become harmful arrogance when based on self-centeredness instead of God. God loves a humble heart, but being humble does not deny our gifts and talents. And humility is not the pursuit of mediocrity.

At Christmas time, jealousy finds its way into our minds. We see the elaborate and classy decorations of our friends, and we want to outdo them. A friend says she is all finished with shopping and wrapping, and we turn a bit green. Someone's spouse presents them with an extravagant gift, and we want attention like that, too. Some people go into debt at Christmas and can't pay it off before the next Christmas appears on the calendar. Christmas is not the time for jealousy or greed. Instead, it is the perfect setting for worship and finding the power of the Savior.

God has given us tools to correct our jealous hearts. Prayer is the first tool. We ask God to purify our hearts as only he can do. The process begins with confession—telling God what he already knows about our actions and thoughts. Internally, we can change our attitude to humility. Externally, we can ask friends to be honest when they see pride and jealousy in our actions. Read Philippians 2:5-11. This passage shows the reason for Christmas. How did Jesus show humility and why? Make a list of reasons to be thankful this Christmas. Give a gift anonymously. Streamline the decorations. Invite friends to your home for a simple supper. Make this the year you celebrate the true meaning of Jesus' birth. What will you do to eliminate pride and jealousy this season?

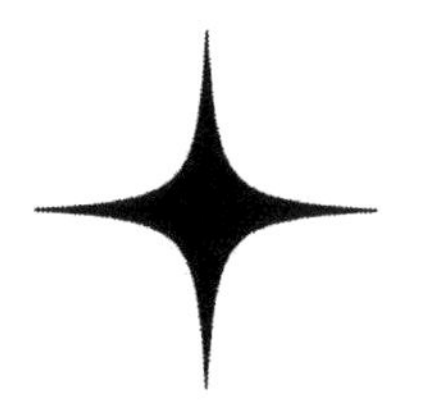

The Jealous Heart Leads to

The Destructive Heart.

~King Herod

Seeing is believing, but sometimes the most real things in the world are the things we can't see.

~The Polar Express

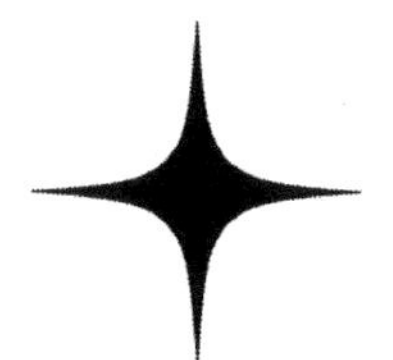

Scribes and Pharisees

The Skeptical Heart

Leads to The Hard Heart

The candle flame flickered in the night, and Nico rubbed his tired eyes. He had pored over the text for hours. The words of the prophet Isaiah, written 700 years before. From the time he was a small boy hearing it read in the synagogue, it had been his favorite. He had committed most of it to memory because Isaiah spoke about the hope for his people.

All day, Nico had been bothered by what he'd seen. It had confused him, and questions filled his mind. Early that morning, he had gone to the temple as usual. He had finished his prayers and was leaving when a young couple with a newborn baby caught his attention. They were talking to the old man, Simeon, who often visited the temple. Simeon took the baby into his arms and cradled him gently. Nico had been curious about the strange look on Simeon's face. He had never seen such pure joy. With a deep love, Simeon looked at the child and spoke. Nico edged closer to the group to hear what he was saying.

"I can die content, for you have fulfilled your promise to me. With my own eyes I have seen your Word, the Savior you sent into the world. He will be glory for your people Israel and the Redemption-Light for all people everywhere."

Suddenly, Anna, the well-known widowed prophetess, who had been worshiping in the temple for more than 80 years, walked up to Simeon, the young couple, and the baby. She began singing loudly and praising God for the child. She danced around, proclaiming to all redemption had come, that the long-awaited Messiah was here.

Nico ran his fingers through his long black beard as he remembered the events. Feelings of shock came over him again. *The Messiah? How could that be true?*

He knew the prophecies about the Messiah. They had all been waiting for him. No one knew when he would arrive, but surely, he wouldn't come like this. He would come as their conquering king, the political leader they needed. He would come as a warrior to conquer Rome and save them from the cruel oppression of the Roman legal system. He would come to lead them to freedom. *Right?*

****

Have you ever believed something wholeheartedly only to discover what you believed wasn't true? It's a difficult position. When our views are challenged, we become skeptical of the information and skeptical of the people giving us the information. Long-held beliefs are difficult to change.

For years, people believed the world was flat. They had every reason to believe it to be true. They thought the earth was a disc floating on a body of water. Some even thought the earth had a domed sky.

The idea of a spherical Earth appeared in ancient Greek philosophy with Pythagoras, but the flat Earth was a widely held belief. Many people for centuries lived and died believing this to be true. Yet, they were wrong. In the early 4th century BC, the spherical Earth was written about by Plato, and around 330, Aristotle provided strong evidence proving the Earth to be round. The thought of the Earth having a round shape gradually spread throughout the world. As knowledge increased and as science progressed, we learned the world was not flat but in fact round. What was widely thought to be true was no longer so.

This knowledge changed the world. Men, no longer fearing they would fall off the edge of the earth, explored and pushed themselves beyond known boundaries. They set off in ships searching for new and unknown lands. The world, as they knew it, expanded, and it would never be the same.

The Skeptical Heart

When Jesus was born, the Jews were led by religious men known as Pharisees. These men were the teachers of the ways of God. They had studied the old books. They knew the law. The Pharisees were convinced they understood the rules and the way people should live if they wanted to follow God fully. The Scribes were experts in the law and could write legal documents. They were learned men and respected as scholars.

The Jews were looking for the Messiah to come. Many expected him to ride in on a horse, like a warrior, armed and ready to deliver the Jewish people from the life of oppression they were experiencing under the Roman Empire. He would come and conquer and release them all from their bondage. The Pharisees and Scribes knew how the Messiah would come.

Or at least they thought they did.

God surprised them all by sending the Messiah, the Savior of the World, not as a conquering warrior but a tiny baby wrapped in swaddling clothes. Born to a young girl from Nazareth of all places.

Why were they skeptical when Jesus came? If anyone should have known baby Jesus was the Messiah, it was the Pharisees and the Scribes. They had studied the Scriptures foretelling his birth.

"Therefore the Lord himself will give you a sign: Behold, the virgin will be with child and will give birth to a son, and will call him Immanuel,"

(Isaiah 7:14 BSB)

"For unto us a child is born, to us a son is given,
and the government will be on his shoulders.
And he will be called Wonderful Counselor,
Mighty God, Everlasting Father, Prince of
Peace."

(Isaiah 9:6 NIV)

Yet they were skeptical. Why didn't they believe? It seems these religious leaders were stuck in their rules. They were obsessed with their laws, obsessed with their ways of thinking, and obsessed with making sure everyone else was doing life their way. They were devoted to the Law of Moses, and they opposed any teaching that wasn't their own. They were right, and anything else was wrong.

Do you like to be right? I do. To a fault. Our family will sit at the table discussing a topic, and all too often a disagreement about some petty, insignificant fact will arise. No one is satisfied until the truth is determined. Someone will pull out their phone and Google it so we can all move on. My daughter has a funny saying, "Every conversation ends with Google." Before the Internet … Oh the disagreements we had.

Years ago, not long into my marriage and before the world wide web, my husband Craig and I were discussing a movie we had seen years before. We disagreed on who played a particular part in the movie. We were both convinced we were right and refused to concede. The discussion went on for days—I know, ridiculous. Finally, Craig, convinced he was right, took me by the hand and led me to the car. He drove to Blockbuster Video, found the movie on the shelf, and turned the case over to see who was listed as playing the role. To my dismay, Craig showed me the name he had fought for so vigorously. He was right, and what I had believed was wrong.

Thankfully, our marriage has grown, and we've matured. Being right is not always the most important. And thank goodness for Google.

The Hard Heart

The Pharisees had to be right, too. When Jesus came and challenged everything the Pharisees knew and believed, their skeptical hearts became hard hearts. They refused to believe God had another plan. Their way was the right way.

Perhaps they had overlooked the passage in Isaiah 55:8, "'For my thoughts are not your thoughts, neither are your ways my ways,' declares the LORD" (NIV).

No one likes to have their beliefs challenged, but with God we need to remember he doesn't fit in our box. He's the Creator, not limited by our human rules. He thinks differently than we do. He continually does the new. There are times God wants to burst out of the box and show us something new and work in a way we never expected.

Hard hearts are also dangerous.

> "But you have a hard and stubborn heart, and so you are making your own punishment even greater on the Day when God's anger and righteous judgments will be revealed."
>
> (Romans 2:5 GNT)

Isn't it interesting how the wise men, Gentiles from a foreign land with curious hearts, confirmed his identity, but the Pharisees, Jews looking for the Messiah to come, didn't see Jesus for who he was? Strange and sad.

Is your heart skeptical and hard? Maybe you think you don't need God. Maybe you think religion is a crutch for the weak. Maybe you are unsure about all this God stuff.

What if it is true? What if he is the Savior? What if he is the Messiah who came to save the world?

The Bible is full of messianic prophecies. Mathematician Peter Stoner calculated the probability of one person fulfilling even a few of the prophecies. The chance of the prophesied Messiah fulfilling only eight of the prophecies is one in 100,000,000,000,000,000 (1 in 10^{17}).

In order to comprehend this staggering probability, Stoner illustrates:

> "... we take 10^{17} silver dollars and lay them on the face of Texas. They will cover the state two feet deep. Now mark one of these silver dollars and stir the whole mass thoroughly. Blindfold a man and tell him that he must pick up one silver dollar and say that this is the right one. What chance would he have of getting the right one?"

If that is the probability of one man fulfilling eight of the prophecies, what are the chances one man could fulfill 48 of the prophecies found in the Old Testament? It's 1 in 10^{157}. In other words, a 1 followed by 157 zeros. However, Jesus didn't just fulfill eight prophecies or even 48 prophecies related to the Messiah. In fact, he fulfilled more than 324. The probability of one man fulfilling 324 prophecies is a number beyond comprehension. Jesus is who he says he is.

Exploring Your Heart

1. Softening Your Hard Heart

Nicodemus was a skeptical Pharisee. In John 3, we learn he was a Pharisee who dared to ask questions. He had seen the miracles of Jesus and heard his teaching, but he was not fully convinced. He had a night encounter with

Jesus where he sought answers to his skepticism. The Scriptures do not tell us if Nicodemus left his meeting with Jesus believing. We do see him later in John 7:51-52, defending Jesus from the attacks of other Pharisees. Following the crucifixion, Nicodemus is mentioned in John 19:39-40 as one of those who helped prepare the body of Jesus for burial, along with Joseph of Arimathea. It appears Nicodemus' hard heart had softened.

Ezekiel 36:26 says, "I will give you a new heart, and a new spirit I will put within you. And I will remove the heart of stone from your flesh and give you a heart of flesh" (ESV). When we open our heart to God's ways, he changes the hard places. Places where we were stubborn, unforgiving, unwilling, and unloving begin to soften.

Do you look at your heart and know you need to change? Try praying this, "God, I'm so grateful You have the power and the desire to soften hard hearts. Show me where my heart is hard, and I ask you to do what is necessary to soften it."

What events or experiences have happened to you that have softened your heart? Thank God and ask him to continue to work on those areas.

2. It's Always Been That Way

Like the Pharisees and Scribes, we can get stuck in a rut, believing something simply because we've always held it to be true.

For example, I once heard a story about a newly married woman who wanted to cook a roast for her new husband. As she prepared the roast for cooking, she cut off both ends.

Her husband was confused and asked, "Why did you do that?"

"That's the way my mom always did it," she replied.

Her husband laughed and said, "That's weird. I don't think my mom ever did that."

The new bride was sure she was supposed to cut off the ends of the roast, so she called her mother to ask about the purpose of this step. Her mother said, "I don't know why you are supposed to cut the ends off. It's the way we've always done it. Let me call your grandmother."

When she called to ask about the reason for cutting the ends of the roast. The grandmother said, "Because it wouldn't fit in my pan."

Sometimes our thoughts and our ways are marred by tradition, bias, and stubbornness. We must open our hearts to the ways of God and the ways he works. Remember the verse from Isaiah? His ways are not our ways.

Can you think of a time you believed something was true only to discover it wasn't true? Can you remember when God worked unusually to teach you something or solve a problem? Write a prayer to God, celebrating the fact he doesn't always fit in the boxes we create for him. Thank him for his creativity and ask him to help you not be skeptical. Take a chance and believe in his work.

3. Embracing a Christmas Heart

God wants to remove the skeptical heart and replace it with a heart believing fully in him.

It is easy to get caught up in the substitute celebrations of Christmas. We highlight Santa, elves, reindeer, gifts, lights, and snowmen instead of Jesus.

Every Christmas, Charles Schwartz's *A Charlie Brown Christmas* is shown on television. The famous cartoon demonstrates how Charlie Brown becomes dispirited upon seeing the commerciality of Christmas. At the end, he can no longer contain his frustration and shouts to his friends, "Can anyone tell me the true meaning of Christmas?" His friend Linus then shares the Christmas story straight from Luke 2.

Approach this Christmas season by refusing to embrace the skeptical heart of the Pharisees. Open your eyes to the beauty and wonder of the miraculous birth of Jesus.

Celebrate letting go of your skepticism by searching for a new Christmas ornament of the nativity. Find one in whatever style you enjoy, or better yet, if you are crafty, make one. Hang it on your tree as a reminder of God continually doing something new and unexpected.

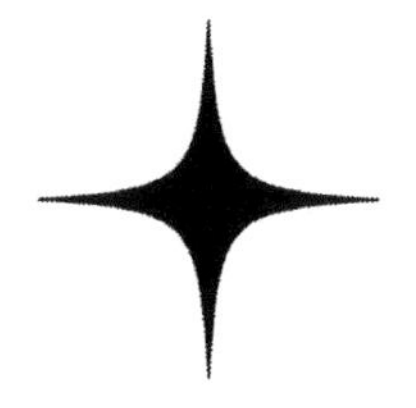

The Skeptical Heart Leads to

The Hard Heart.

~The Scribes and Pharisees

Christmas is not as much about opening our presents as opening our hearts.

~Janice Maeditere

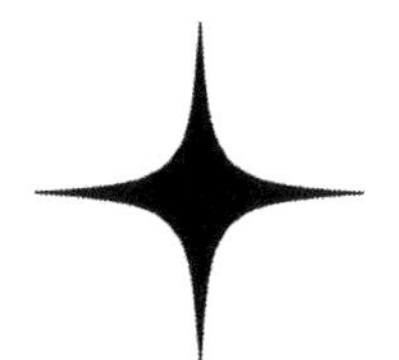

A Manger Heart Leads to the Savior

How about your heart? The answer matters. Getting our heart harmonious with God is the key lesson we learned from the characters of Christmas. If our heart is out of tune, we won't see the true meaning of Christ coming to earth to save us from our sins, and we will miss the blessings God has ready for us.

For some of us, circumstances have damaged our hearts like the people in the story.

- Zechariah's disappointment because he and Elizabeth did not have a child caused him to be reluctant to believe even when he saw a vision straight from God.
- Elizabeth's barrenness brought shame in her society, her broken heart laid bare in its pain.

- The Innkeeper's hectic schedule seared his heart so he couldn't see the world's greatest event.
- For hundreds of years, religious leaders waited for prophecies to be fulfilled, and the delays filled their hearts with skepticism.
- Herod allowed his own insecurities and self-centeredness to generate jealousy in his heart.

Others have positive qualities in their heart.

- Mary's heart was ready to answer yes to anything God wanted to ask.
- Joseph's kindness allowed him to see beyond the potential scandal to the truth of God.
- A life of obscurity and time to develop deep understanding gave the shepherds a keen willingness to hear the good news.
- Wise men who studied astrology with curiosity were willing to search the ancient records to satisfy their questions about the unusual star.

But the Christmas story changes hearts.

If you believe, your heart goes to a higher level of faith and wonder at the grace of God. If you allow your damaged heart to rule, the Christmas story leads to a path of disobedience, selfishness, emptiness, and destruction.

We have often thought about that night in the stable. It can't have been the sterile environment we would want for our baby. It was dark and smelly as Joseph worked to clear the feeding trough. Mary endured the pain and fear of a young girl in first-time childbirth.

And we've wished the manger could talk, giving us an eyewitness view of the most glorious moment in history.

Imagine the picture painted by this makeshift cradle. The manger was unoccupied. Open. Ready for the babe.

Examine your heart. Is your heart ready for the babe of Christmas? Do you need hope? Accepting Jesus will remake your reluctant, or broken, or busy, or jealous, or skeptical heart. Allowing his control in your life will transform you and take you to a new spiritual level—even if your heart is ready or kind or eager or curious.

Decide now to welcome the Savior into your heart.

Will you make your heart a manger?

~Cherry and Karen

The Christmas miracle will take place in your heart and then in your life.

~Karen Porter

Meet the Authors

Karen Porter and Cherry McGregor are a mother-daughter team who love working together on projects and gathering family and friends. Each year at Christmas, they bake more than 6,000 cookies to raise funds for a beloved school in India.

****

Karen Porter is an international retreat and seminar speaker and a successful businesswoman. She is the author of eight books including *I'll Bring the Chocolate: Satisfying a Woman's Cravings for Friendship and Faith* and *If You Give a Girl A Giant.*

Karen spends most of her time coaching aspiring writers and speakers and training communicators across the globe.

Karen and her husband, George, own Bold Vision Books, a traditional Christian small press. She serves on the board of several non-profit organizations.

Karen says her marriage to George is her greatest achievement, but she'd love to talk to you about her five grandchildren. In her spare time, Karen continues her life-long quest to find the perfect purse.

Cherry McGregor is known for her creative genius and warm hospitality. Her life is full—raising kids and managing the books of the family business.

At her church, she is a key team member for event planning, leads a hospitality team, and is a teacher of a new member's class.

Cherry has a Bachelors Degree in Biomedical Science from Texas A&M and holds a Doctorate Degree in Chiropractic Medicine. She is a lover of basketball, college football, family board games, and all things Texas A&M.

She is married to Craig, a local dentist and has three children, Garrett, Gracen, and Gabriella. And in her spare time she's mamma to a big black lab.

Notes

In the dialogue sections for each character in the Christmas story, some conversations are quoted from Psalms, Isaiah, Deuteronomy, Luke, and Matthew from the NIV, NLT, and TPT.

Bible Versions and Translations Used

Made in the USA
Monee, IL
18 November 2022

a2e5871f-a1c3-4336-8a5e-ad240cd89182R01